Children of

CW01454608

Connecting School and Parish

An **ALIVE-O 1-4** Handbook
for Classroom Visitations

The glory of God is people fully alive.
St Irenaeus

Compiled by Eleanor Gormally

VERITAS

Published 2001 by
Veritas Publications
7-8 Lower Abbey Street
Dublin 1

ISBN 1 85390 584 4

Acknowledgements
'Columba' (p. 48) and 'Thanks "Bee" to God' (p. 153) by Clare Maloney.
All other poems as credited in the text.

Cover design by Colette Dower
Cover illustration by Jeanette Dunne
Origination by Accuplate Ltd, Dublin
Printed in Ireland by Betaprint Ltd, Dublin

Contents

Foreword

The greatest challenges facing the Church at this time are those of evangelisation and catechesis. For some people the gospel needs to be presented at its most basic level. For others what is required is ongoing formation that builds on the faith that is already there. This work of evangelisation and catechesis will be most effective where different agencies work together in harmony. The primary school classroom offers a golden opportunity for such partnership in faith formation. Priests and other parish personnel who visit the school are in a position to support the work of the teachers and to foster deeper links between school and parish. It goes without saying that familiarity with the catechetical programme being used in the classroom is vital if the time spent in the classroom is to bear most fruit. The parish representative who has a good grasp of the programme will have more confidence when it comes to presenting it in the classroom. Given the many commitments most priests have, it may not be possible for many of them to familiarise themselves with the whole of the *Alive-O* programme. Whatever their situation, this volume prepared by Eleanor Gormally is a welcome gift. It offers a road map of the first four years of the *Alive-O* programme and selects themes from it that can be used through the year at school visits. For the visitor to the school who wants to link in with the prayer of the children, introduce them to the great themes in the liturgical seasons of the year and deepen their appreciation of the sacraments, the material in this book will be invaluable. It follows that those who take the trouble to study this volume are equipping themselves to be more effective partners with teachers in passing on the faith to the children whose sense of wonder opens them out to the wonder of God's presence in their young lives.

✠ Martin Drennan

The Beauty of a Child

In the face of a child,
see the beauty of God,
of the clear graceful wonder,
of life and creation.

In the eyes of the child
see the seeking of love,
the want of affection
of those whom they love.

There is no fear of exposure
in their sharing of joy;
for they have not yet encountered
life's pain or its wounds.
>   *Brother Cornelius Kearney*

When, as adults, we cross the threshold of a school, we cross into a world apart – a world that moves to its own rhythm and time frame; a world that is shaped by the spontaneity, energy and learning of children. The school environment brings us into the company of children with an immediacy and a vibrancy that cannot easily be ignored. When drawn into this rhythm the 'visitor' is invited to absorb the atmosphere, to tap into the movement unique to the school day, to engage with the teachers, but most of all he/she is invited into the presence of children.

Some of us enter into and connect with the world of children with ease and enthusiasm. For more of us, however, the school has become an unfamiliar place, unvisited since our childhood days.

This book is directed to priests and other parish personnel who venture across the classroom threshold. It is hoped that the book might help to deepen and enrich the experience of those who have already come to know and value the benefits of entering this world. But it is also directed to those priests and parish personnel who, for whatever reason, have yet to discover the joy and wonder of engaging with primary-school children. It is hoped that the guidelines below may offer a sort of bridge between the adult world and the child's world.

The classroom can provide a unique opportunity to converse with young children and tap into their dreams and aspirations, their concerns and excitements, their joys and hopes. Young children are by nature full of awe and wonder, they are free and spontaneous, not yet restricted or limited by life's conventions and experiences. An overriding capacity to be themselves, to take life at face value, to engage openly with those with whom they feel secure is a dominant characteristic of young children, and contributes to the creation of an ideal climate in which to participate in the children's faith development.

The aim of this booklet then is to offer a kind of road-map through the first four years of *Alive-O* that hopefully will encourage priests and parish personnel to venture into the world of the classroom, discover the treasures that await them and engage with the faith journey of primary-school children.

The Aim of Religious Education

The aim of religious education in the primary school is to foster and deepen the children's faith. People of faith perceive themselves and their world in a special way. Faith is our response to God's self-communication to us through revelation. God's initiative is a gift, an invitation. The response we make is our choice, our decision. It is a response that no one can make on behalf of another, neither can it be forced from anyone. What is possible, however, is the creation of a context wherein people have the opportunity to become aware of God's invitation, to hear God's word and to explore how best they can respond in their own lives. *Alive-O* seeks to enable children to grow as people of faith in the hope that they will be capable of giving an account of the faith that is within them, to say what they believe and why. This familiarity with the content of faith is achieved gradually as the children move from class to class, and as their ability to understand difficult language and concepts increases.

Alive-O seeks, therefore, to be a resource for those who accompany children on their faith journey. Many people influence the religious education of children, directly and indirectly, at personal and institutional levels: parents/guardians and significant adults in the home, teachers, priests and diocesan advisers, parish personnel and the wider Christian community. As children grow and develop in their awareness of the action and presence of God in their lives they will need continued guidance, direction and affirmation from home, school and parish. It is true to say that the primary religious educators of the child are the parents/guardians in the home. They are the ones who are responsible for the nurture and care of the child. They are the ones who, at Baptism, in presenting their child before the Christian community, agreed to raise their child as a member of that community. In the past it was from the home that children learned the language of faith and saw it reflected in the lives of people around them. However, we can no longer assume or take for granted the faith patterns of the past. Now more than ever we need to continue to explore new and creative ways of reawakening in parents/guardians and in children themselves a sense of the transcendent dimension in their lives. Religious educators need to be persistent in their endeavour to discover, and indeed rediscover, ways of making real for themselves and for others, a true sense of belonging to a community that professes that Jesus is Lord, that he is alive and active in our individual and collective lives. Children need to be helped to become people of faith, people who see the world through the eyes of faith and situate their everyday experiences in the context of a belief in a loving and compassionate God. In today's fast-changing, secular-dominated culture this is not always an easy task. However, when supportive structures are set in place between school and home, between school and parish and between school, home and parish, the isolation of individual roles can become diminished and the fruits of partnership increased.

What is *Alive-O*?

Alive-O is a re-presentation of the *Children of God* series. It offers age-appropriate programmes for Junior Infants/Primary One (*Alive-O*), Senior Infants/Primary Two (*Alive-O 2*), First Class/Primary Three (*Alive-O 3)* and Second Class/Primary Four (*Alive-O 4*). The title *Alive-O* reflects the overriding aim of religious education, namely, to enable people to become fully alive to the presence of God in themselves, in others, in the Church and in the world around them. A teacher's kit accompanies each year. The following elements are contained in each kit:

Teacher's Manual
The best way to gain an understanding of *Alive-O* is through the teacher's manuals. Each manual contains all of the material to be taught to the children over the course of the year. The content is clearly laid out and divided according to the terms of the school year. A glance at the Table of Contents of any given year will provide an overview of the scope and sequence of individual lessons. For each week there is a lesson, which contains resources in the following areas: story, song, prayer, art, poetry, activities and classroom conversations. The content is always situated within a sound theological, scriptural, moral and catechetical framework. It provides teachers with the background material and methodology necessary for the effective communication of the Christian message to young children. It can also be a resource to others such as priests or other parish personnel who visit the classrooms regularly. A theological background is given for each lesson.

For a fuller and more in-depth understanding of the *Alive-O* programme the Introduction to the teacher's manual is essential reading. Grounded in the understanding that 'Faith is a personal act – the free response of the human person to the initiative of God who reveals himself' (*CCC*, 166), the introduction outlines the doctrinal, scriptural, sacramental and moral background to the content of each programme. It is strongly recommended, therefore, that the Introduction to the *Alive-O* teacher's manuals be studied in advance of any visit to the classroom.

Pupil Book

A pupil book accompanies each year. The pupil book is a colourful and child-centred resource. It is designed to capture the child's imagination and attention in a way that will help consolidate the core concepts and ideas that are being explored. The pupil book can provide an excellent starting point for conversation with the children. It also contains notes for parents, the formal prayers the children are learning and some simple prayers written in a language that children can easily understand and remember.

Worksheets/Workbooks

The kit contains a set of photocopiable worksheets, one for each lesson. Alternatively, these worksheets are available in the form of a workbook. The workbook/worksheets involve the children in active learning. Through drawing, writing and colouring the children are invited to explore themes in a fun and age-appropriate manner. These worksheets are also found in the Resource Pack. The Resource Pack also includes Parent Information Sheets and Parish Information Sheets.

Posters

A set of twelve posters is available as an optional resource. These are A1-size reproductions of some of the pictures in the pupil text. They have the potential to provide a focal point for classroom discussion or for prayer. Not every classroom might invest in posters. Where they are bought, however, as part of the *Alive-O* kit, they can proffer the classroom visitor with an immediate and attractive stimulus for discussion with the children.

Video

Each kit contains a video. The video is an integral part of *Alive-O*. It seeks to journey with the children through the year, taking the same path as the teacher's text. The video visually explores through music, song, movement, story, ritual and prayer the core themes of the year. It is usually divided into clearly named sections and is accompanied by guidelines for viewing. Looking at the video with the children can encourage them to engage in active watching and listening, leading to the development of reflective skills. It can initiate and encourage a different kind of chatting and discussion as visitor and pupil, together, interact with the material.

CD/Tapes

Each lesson in *Alive-O* contains at least one song. The songs serve to develop the theme of the lesson. Children love to listen to songs. They also love to sing and perform for others and to demonstrate their skills and expertise. A visitor to the classroom can expect a delightful treat as children give of their best in full voice. Alternatively, a visitor gifted in music may wish to share his/her musical talents with the children. The music for a particular year is recorded on both cassette and CD.

Alive-O (Junior Infants/Primary One) and *Alive-O 2* (Senior Infants/Primary Two)

Alive-O and *Alive-O 2* focus on the world of the infant child. At this stage four- to six-year-old children are taking tentative steps away from the familiar world of home and are entering the larger, unfamiliar world of the school. *Alive-O* reflects this point of transition that children are at. It seeks to help the children to become aware of their innate uniqueness and to come to appreciate how their uniqueness is expressed in who they are and what they do. As such, each child is a unique expression of God's image in the world. *Alive-O* affirms and treasures that uniqueness. Each year the age and development of the child is taken into consideration and the Christian story is presented in accordance with the child's capacity and life experience. When we look at the natural world around us we see many signs of God's action, power and wisdom; the cycle of the seasons, the grandeur of nature and the mystery of new life all speak of the power and mystery of God. Lessons on autumn, spring, winter and summer offer the children an opportunity to tap into the mystery and wonder of God in the world around them.

The emergence of the young child from her/his egocentric world is a gradual one. Slowly the child begins to become aware of those around her and to see others, not as servers of her own desires but as individuals who themselves have needs and rights. *Alive-O 2* continues to affirm the children in their own worth and gently nudges them towards an appreciation of others and the wider world around them. Lessons like 'Together Again', 'Getting Along Together', 'Let's Celebrate', 'They Care For Me' offer the children an opportunity to explore the interdependence that exists between all individuals. In so doing, the process of awakening an awareness of the tension between the 'I' and the Christian call to live in relationship with others is begun and a foundation towards an understanding of the concept of community is being laid. Over the course of the year the children are drawn into the cycle and rhythm of the Church seasons. They listen to the story of the first Christmas and celebrate the joy of the Easter experience in song and prayer, drama and ritual. The Introduction to the teacher's manual offers a more detailed account of the doctrinal content for each year.

Characteristics of Four- to Six-Year-Olds
Some people's line of work may draw them more frequently into adult interaction and conversation. For others, their day-to-day work may bring them into the company of children. However, when planning to meet young

children in the more formal world of the school setting it might be useful to be aware of some of the characteristics of infant children that *Alive-O* takes into consideration when developing core content and exploring experiences with them.

Four- to six-year-olds:
- are often more open than adults to being excited by their own unique gifts and talents. The notion 'I am special' rests easily with them;
- are fascinated by the world of nature. They have an innate sense of mystery and a tremendous openness to wonder and awe;
- learn through their senses. Their span of attention is short and can be best maintained when they are actively involved in whatever they are learning;
- can vary greatly in their capacity to express themselves orally. In chatting to them about what it is they are learning it is best to offer them a variety of options. Some children will eagerly respond to the invitation to tell a story. For other children, it might be more appropriate to ask them to draw a picture;
- learn through play. Children negotiate their relationship with the space around them through play, they express their creativity freely and they put their own shape on the world around them. Play is a wonderful tool in helping children to experience, explore and empathise. It is particularly powerful when followed with reflection through chat or drawing;
- are egocentric by nature. They see and judge everything around them in terms of themselves and their own experience. In interacting with children of this age it is important to begin to help them to take on the perspective of others and to appreciate that other people have needs;
- are influenced by the behaviour of adults that surround them. They have the capacity to imitate adult behaviour and to absorb the attitudes of significant adults, even when they don't fully understand them.

Alive-O 3 (First Class/Primary Three) and *Alive-O 4* (Second Class/Primary Four)

Alive-O 3 and *Alive-O 4* explore a variety of themes such as journey, belonging, interconnectedness and interdependence. Over the course of the year the children are helped to develop a sense of identity and belonging by reflecting on what it is like to begin a new year; to take part in the rhythm of the school day; to watch the changing seasons of the year; to be part of the dynamic that makes up a class. They are helped to see the interrelatedness between all things, that each of us exists within a complex web of relationships that connect us to a sense of ourselves, to those around us, to the world in which we live and, ultimately, to God.

Alive-O 3 continues to introduce the children to Jesus, Son of God, a process begun in *Alive-O* and *Alive-O 2*. *Alive-O 3* presents Jesus as someone who consistently journeyed with others – even the outcast, the sinner and the marginalised. He was there to share his stories, his food and his vision for the Kingdom of God with those who had ears to hear. He called people to go forth beyond their own individual world to work together towards the creation and realisation of a world of peace, love, equality and justice. In *Alive-O 4* the children explore how Jesus set out to share his spirit of life with those around him. They reflect on how it animated his relationship with others and come to appreciate how central it was to how he related to God the Father.

Characteristics of Six- to Eight-Year-Olds
The move from the Infant/Primary One and Primary Two classrooms to First and Second Class/Primary Three and Primary Four marks yet another significant stage in the growth and development of the life of a young child. They may be entering a more formal environment, with a new teacher and maybe a longer school day. They may no longer consider themselves the 'babies' in the school. They may see themselves as entering the 'big' school. They may feel more grown up and confident.

In order to be able to tap into the stage of development that the six- to eight-year-old is at, it might be useful to be aware of some of the characteristics that *Alive-O* takes into consideration when developing and exploring core content with this age-group.

Six- to eight-year-olds:
- love to discover new things about themselves and the world around them. They are open to new ideas and can be easily motivated to self-directed learning;
- have a natural capacity for awe and wonder. They are fascinated by the world of nature. They have a sense of mystery;
- learn best through active participation and involvement in the learning process;
- are moving beyond their egocentric world and are beginning to become aware of the needs and perspectives of others. They have a strong desire to belong; class and friendship groups are extremely important to them;
- need the love, affirmation and support of significant adults if they are to develop a positive sense of their own worth. It is through their experience of the love and care of others that they will come to understand and celebrate the love and compassion of God.

How to Use this Book

The aim of this book is to give the reader a pathway through the first four years of *Alive-O* that will be helpful when visiting the classroom and interacting with children at the junior end of the primary school, i.e. Junior Infants to Second Class/Primary One to Primary Four.

Selection of material is a necessary task to a compilation of this nature. The task of selection is not an easy one, especially when one is faced with such a wide variety of material to choose from across the four different years. While certain material will be highlighted for attention, everything cannot be chosen.

Any selection is limited in itself but it is hoped that the selection presented here will offer the reader a satisfactory 'taste' of *Alive-O*, enabling him/her to gain an understanding of and familiarisation with the various programmes. Perhaps this 'taste' will encourage some to explore *Alive-O* more fully by reading the teacher's manuals, thereby experiencing at greater depth the scope and sequence of each programme.

The book has been divided into five separate sections. Each section is clearly delineated.

Section One: Setting the Scene
Section One offers some helpful hints on how to plan your school visit; outlines the scope and sequence for each of the four *Alive-O* years; explains the structure of the *Alive-O* lesson, and offers guidelines for multi-class situations.

Section Two: Alive-O *Through the Liturgical Year*
Section Two presents a selection of lessons/themes to choose from during the year as well as helpful hints for classroom visits. With the exception of lessons marking the beginning and the ending of the school year, the liturgical events of the Church year form the main focus of this section (Feast of All Saints and All Souls, Advent, Christmas, Ash Wednesday, Lent, Easter, May – the month of Mary). In all, eight themes are outlined and explored.

Section Three: Saints Alive-O!
Each year the children are introduced to at least one saint. Section Three gathers together the stories of the lives of Saints Brigid, Patrick, Columba (Colmcille) and Gobnait. This section looks at each saint individually and offers suggestions as to how the classroom visitor might make best use of the material during a school visit.

Section Four: Prayer Services
On three occasions in the school year the opportunity exists for the teacher to invite parents/guardians of the children to join with the class in prayer. The Prayer Services are centred on the themes that the children are exploring

in class. The local parish clergy are also invited to participate in these prayer times. Section Four explains the Prayer Services and places them in the context of *Alive-O*. This section also includes some examples of their format and structure, for those who may wish to participate in them.

Section Five: Sacramental Catechesis

Section Five offers a quick overview to the sacramental lessons on Baptism, Reconciliation and Eucharist. It offers suggestions on what the visitor might focus on during a school visit.

Sections Six: Liturgical Links

Section Six offers some ideas on how *Alive-O* might be integrated with the Sunday liturgies. It also offers a series of grids outlining the scripture stories and formal prayers with which the children are familiar.

Section One: Setting the Scene

Planning Your School/Class Visit

Planning school visits takes time and effort. However, time spent on advance planning may help to increase the effectiveness of the visit as well as heighten the enjoyment of the visit for you and for the children.

As the circumstances of each parish and diocese will vary in relation to the size and number of primary schools and also the number of personnel available for school visits, it is suggested that you take the following key questions into consideration when organising your schedule.

How can I best manage my time?
Know the amount of time you have for school visits each year. Be realistic about the time you will spend in each class. Remember that time well spent with the children will help forge links between the school and the parish and will help to build a positive rapport with the children. The amount of time at your disposal will determine the scope of your visit. From the menu of suggestions offered in this book, choose what best fits into your particular time frame. Keeping your visit focused will save time and prove more successful for you and the children.

In visiting a range of classes, is there a common theme I can focus on?
There are several common themes that can be focused on. The beginning and ending of the school year is one example. The liturgical seasons of Advent, Christmas, Lent and Easter are another example. While the slant given to the theme will vary from class to class, staying with the same theme across a few of the classes may help structure your advance preparation.

How do I choose a theme?
Read through the themes and their accompanying objectives offered in this book and see what ones suit you best. Look up the relevant teacher's manuals for greater insight and detail. Remember that each term offers different options. There is plenty of material and lesson elements to choose from: Story, Song, Chatting, Art, Pupil Book, Video, Prayertime. (These will be explained fully in 'Exploring the *Alive-O* Lesson' below.)

When planning your visit it is important to choose the aspect that best suits your situation. In making your choice it might be useful to consider your own particular talents and giftedness. If, for example, you love story and story-telling, you might choose to make *Story* the focus of your visit. On the other hand, you may be gifted with a singing voice, in which case you may wish to sing a *Song* for or with the children. (All the songs are available on

CD/tape.) Discussing opinions and sharing ideas with young children may be your strong point. The *Chattings* offer wonderful opportunities to tap into children's unique way of reflecting on their experiences. Those with a flare for technology may find the *Video* a very useful tool in exploring themes with the children. Children are so used to passively viewing TV and videos that watching the *Alive-O* video sections with the children can provide an excellent opportunity to invite children to become active viewers. Finally, prayer is central to religious education. A school visit should, where possible, leave some space for prayer with the children. *Alive-O* offers a great variety of ways of praying with children. In each of the eight themes a particular *Prayertime* from the relevant *Alive-O* programme will be given. Some people may like to use this Prayertime with all the classes to mark the beginning or the end of the visit. However, people are free to use whatever prayer format they choose.

Have I visited the class(es) before? What was the focus of that visit?
You might find it useful to keep a short record of the school visits. While you may not remember exactly what you chatted about in your last visit, the children certainly will!

Exploring the *Alive-O* Lesson

Each *Alive-O* lesson is structured in a characteristic way. Each lesson is divided into five parts, one for each day of the week. A brief overview of the lesson is available in the teacher's manual. Each lesson contains core elements: Song, Story, Poetry, Chatting, Art, Music, Workbook/Worksheet, Video, Prayertime. Each lesson is structured so as to offer maximum aid to the teacher. It would be unrealistic to expect a visitor to the classroom to have the same familiarity with or knowledge of the lessons as the class teacher. However, a basic awareness of certain elements would be of enormous benefit when choosing a focus for your visit. Elements such as Story, Song, Chatting, Video and Prayertime all offer a rich menu from which to choose.

Story
Listening to and telling stories is an important part of the process of every *Alive-O* lesson. Children love stories. Stories and poems have the capacity to explore abstractions in terms of images and interpersonal experiences. A good story is a mirror that shows us the heights and the depths of human experience, and in doing so gives us the opportunity to view our own experience at a safe distance. Through story, children are helped to come to terms with and understand their own experience. If we allow the stories we tell to evoke the children's own stories, we can help them to articulate their experience and to begin to put shape on their world. In the Christian

tradition, story-telling is not an innovation. Jesus told stories that forced the people of his day to take stock of themselves and their relationships with others, the world and God. Through his stories he challenged and encouraged them to re-evaluate the direction of their lives in the light of the values of God's kingdom.

Most lessons in *Alive-O* contain at least one story. Telling or retelling a story to children can be a wonderful way to access their joys and fears, their attitudes and values, their hopes and expectations. Frequently a conversation begun through the images and form of a story can open doors to a variety of concerns central to the lives and hearts of young children. For easy access to stories addressed in this book, the full text is given. During your visit you might like to tell/read a story to the class. Alternatively, you could invite them to tell you a story.

Chatting
Each lesson contains a number of 'chatting' opportunities. Some of these chattings focus on the story of the lesson, some focus on an aspect of an activity that the children may be involved in, while others might focus on the pupil book or on the children's own life experience. The purpose of these chattings is to engage the children in sincere and relevant conversation with their peers and with the teacher. The chattings are an ideal way for a visitor to gain an insight into the children's view of the world as well as being an effective tool in recalling and remembering what the children have learnt in class and how they have integrated the learning with their everyday lives. The suggestions in Section Two offer pointers for discourse should you choose this element as the focus of your visit.

Song
Each lesson in *Alive-O* contains at least one song. The songs are related to the theme and content of the lessons for which they were intended. The songs seek to explore in words, music and rhythm the spirit of the lesson. They are one of many ways in which *Alive-O* helps the children to reflect on and to remember what they have learnt. The songs are available on CD and tape. Depending on your musical talent you might like to sing a song for the children. Alternatively, you could sing with them or get them to perform for you. Whichever manner you choose, there will always be plenty of scope to explore and discuss the meaning of the song with the children. The words of the songs are found in the teacher's manual or, in the case of *Alive-O 3* and *Alive-O 4*, in the Resource Pack.

Video
A video accompanies each teacher's kit. The video gathers together in visual form the central themes of the year. Many lessons have a section of video to

enhance the work. The video is clearly divided into sections for easy access. Children love to watch videos. Using the video in religious education gives adults a wonderful occasion to encourage active viewing in the children. It also offers a context for dialogue between the visitor and the children. When using the video with the children it is essential to have reviewed the relevant section prior to the classroom visit. Remember to check the availability of a video recorder before choosing this particular element.

Art
Each lesson usually contains several suggestions whereby the children have the opportunity to become engaged in a creative and imaginative way with a given theme. The ever-changing world of the child needs art as a means of self-expression. Through their paintings and drawings children are allowed to express their reactions and fears, their joys and attitudes in a way that often goes beyond the scope of words. Children love to see their work acknowledged and affirmed. You might like to invite the children to show and to talk about their artwork. Any chat about artwork should always be done in a non-judgemental manner.

Prayertime
Prayer is central to any religious education programme. Prayer forms an integral part of *Alive-O*. Children's faith in God is fostered through prayer. Prayer is one of the most important ways that children can learn to express this faith. It is essential, therefore, to develop in the children from an early age the sense that God is always listening and interested in what we have to say. It is important that they come to know God as someone who cares about them, who knows them by name, who has counted the hairs on their head. *Alive-O* seeks to help children to know God as someone who gave them the gift of life, who is interested in their well-being and who sustains the gift of life in them. *Alive-O* encourages the children to pray at certain times throughout the school day – when they come to school in the morning; when they leave at the end of the day; before they eat their lunch; during the Religion lesson. Specific Prayertimes are outlined for each day of the week. When you visit the classroom you might like to pray with the children using one of the lesson Prayertimes. Prayer should be an essential element in classroom visits.

Scope and Sequence

To plan effectively for your visit to the classroom it is useful to be able to see at a glance the sequence of a particular year's work. For this reason the Table of Contents for each of the four years has been reproduced below. The contents pages can help situate the individual lessons within the particular context of each term and within the general context of the year. The developmental connection between the various *Alive-O* programmes can also be seen. It is hoped that the overview might tempt the reader to dip into other lessons/themes not chosen in this specific collection.

Note: The lessons in bold print are the lessons reviewed in this compilation. The page references also apply to this book.

Alive-O

Term One

Lesson 1	Starting School
Lesson 2	Getting to Know You
Lesson 3	**Settling In (p. 23)**
Lesson 4	Here We Are
Lesson 5	My World in Autumn
Lesson 6	Me in Autumn
Lesson 7	Celebrating Change
Lesson 8	**Hallowe'en (p. 39)**
Lesson 9	Belonging
Lesson 10	How Do I Belong?
Lesson 11	This is Where I Belong
Lesson 12	We Belong to God
Lesson 13	**Simeon and Anna Wait (p. 57)**
Lesson 14	**Mary and Joseph Wait (p. 57/134)**
Lesson 15	**Jesus is Born (p. 82)**

Term Two

Lesson 1	My World in Winter
Lesson 2	Me in Winter
Lesson 3	**We Celebrate Saint Brigid (p. 148)**
Lesson 4	Thank You, God, For Me
Lesson 5	Celebrating Me
Lesson 6	**Families Celebrate (p. 96)**
Lesson 7	**A Place to Celebrate (p. 99)**
Lesson 8	My World in Spring
Lesson 9	Me in Spring
Lesson 10	**Easter (p. 115)**

Term Three

Lesson 1	Food is Good
Lesson 2	The Food we Eat
Lesson 3	We Eat Together
Lesson 4	My World in Summer
Lesson 5	Me in Summer
Lesson 6	Holidays
Lesson 7	**Alive-O (p. 145)**

Alive-O 2

Term One

Lesson 1	School Starts
Lesson 2	Together Again
Lesson 3	I Can Feel
Lesson 4	**Getting Along Together (p. 27)**
Lesson 5	Autumn
Lesson 6	Autumn Colours
Lesson 7	Let's Celebrate
Lesson 7	**Let's Remember (p. 45)**
Lesson 8	Hallowe'en
Lesson 9	Caring
Lesson 10	They Care For Me
Lesson 11	I Care For Them
Lesson 12	God Cares For Us
Lesson 13	**Preparing (p. 63)**
Lesson 14	**Preparing for the Birth of Jesus (p. 63)**
Lesson 15	**Celebrating the Birth of Jesus (p. 86)**

Term Two

Lesson 1	Winter – A Time To Rest
Lesson 2	Winter
Lesson 3	**Peace Around Me (Saint Brigid) (p. 148)**
Lesson 4	Peace Within Me
Lesson 5	Special Things
Lesson 6	**Special Places (p. 105)**
Lesson 7	**Saint Patrick (p. 148)**
Lesson 8	New Beginnings
Lesson 9	Spring
Lesson 10	**Easter (p. 119)**

Term Three

Lesson 1	Water is Good
Lesson 2	Water is Fun
Lesson 3	Water is God's Gift
Lesson 4	**I Want a Word (p. 137)**
Lesson 5	Summer Light
Lesson 6	Hurray For Summer
Lesson 7	**Alive-O (p. 145)**

The Multi-Class Situation

In the majority of cases the classes that are visited will be single-class groupings. However, for some the multi-class situation (i.e. two-, three- and four-class groupings) will be the dominant experience. The following outlines the multi-class scenario, describes some of the preferred options that teachers adopt and indicates how a visit to such classrooms might be managed.

Two-Class Situation
A two-class situation arises when Junior Infants/Primary One and Senior Infants/Primary Two are taught by the same teacher. When handling the Religious Education programmes the usual practice adopted by teachers is to teach from one programme each year and to alternate them every second year. Before your visit it is advisable to check with the class teacher as to which *Alive-O* is currently being taught. When you have this information you can then follow the suggestions pertinent to the particular programme being taught as outlined in this book.

Three-Class Situation
In a three-class situation (e.g. Junior Infants/Primary One, Senior Infants/ Primary Two and First Class/Primary Three) teachers usually decide to teach two *Alive-O* programmes in a given year to two separate groupings – group one being an individual class (e.g. First Class/Primary Three) and group two being a combination of the two remaining classes (e.g. Junior Infants/ Primary One and Senior Infants/Primary Two). Following through on the example given above, the teacher would in this case be teaching *Alive-O* or *Alive-O 2* to Junior Infants/Primary One and Senior Infants/Primary Two (alternated every second year) and *Alive-O 3* to First Class/Primary Three. Before your visit find out what combination of classes the teacher has and what system she/he has developed for her/his classroom. A visit to this classroom will mean having to juggle with two programmes. Again, once you know what *Alive-O* programmes to fucus on the guidelines given here should offer you plenty of scope. It might be helpful to choose a theme that is common to all classes.

Four-Class Situation
The four-class situation (e.g. Junior Infants/Primary One, Senior Infants/Primary Two, First Class/Primary Three and Second Class/Primary Four) is the most challenging of all the multi-class situations. For this compilation the system outlined in *Alive-O 1-4 in Multi-class Situations: A Teacher's Guide* (Veritas Publications, 2000) is being followed. This guide suggests that the teacher teach all four classes as one group. To facilitate this *Alive-O 1-4 in Multi-class Situations: A Teacher's Guide* has devised a system whereby certain programmes are paired and integrated together, offering a

four-year cycle: *Alive-O* with *Alive-O 3* (Parts 1 and 2) and *Alive-O 2* with *Alive-O 4* (Parts 1 and 2). Combining the programmes in this way ensures that while the sequence and order of the *Alive-O* lessons may differ from that of the single-class situation, the children are guaranteed to have access to the content of all four programmes by the time they leave Second Class/Primary Four. In planning a visit to a two-teacher school it would be helpful to discuss with the teacher the system she/he is adopting, bearing in mind that teachers explore options that best suit their particular contexts. It would also be useful to familiarise yourself with the guidlelines laid out in *Alive-O 1-4 in Multi-class Situations: A Teacher's Guide.*

It is not possible in this book to present detailed suggestions that cover the entire *Alive-O* four-year multi-class cycle. However, what can be offered is a grid highlighting the eight themes selected for this compilation, placing them in the context of the four-year cycle as given in *Alive-O 1-4 in Multi-class Situations: A Teacher's Guide.* Page references to the guide are indicated for easy access to options and suggestions. It is important to remember that *Alive-O 1-4 in Multi-class Situations: A Teacher's Guide* must always be used in conjunction with the relevant teacher's manual. The grid below outlines the teacher's manual, Term (T) and Lesson (L) number where the particular lesson can be found. The page references apply to *Alive-O 1-4 in Multi-class Situations: A Teacher's Guide (Guide).*

Theme	*Year One*	*Year Two*	*Year Three*	*Year Four*
1. Beginning the new school year	*Alive-O* T1L1 Starting School *Guide* p. 5	*Alive-O 2* T2L2 Together Again *Guide* p. 54	*Alive-O 3* T1L5 We Belong Together *Guide* p. 93	*Alive-O 2* T1L1 School Starts *Guide* p. 138
2. Hallowe'en/ November	*Alive-O 3* T1L6 We Remember Together *Guide* p. 16	*Alive-O 2* T1L7 Let's Remember *Guide* p. 59	*Alive-O* T1L8 Hallowe'en *Guide* p. 101	*Alive-O 4* T1L6 The Feast of All Saints *Guide* p. 147
3. Advent	*Alive-O 3* T1L13/14 One Moment *Guide* p. 26 Watching, Waiting, Wondering *Guide* p. 28	*Alive-O 4* T1L12/13 The People who Walked in Darkness *Guide* p. 67 From Darkness to Light *Guide* p. 69	*Alive-O* T1L13/14 Simeon and Anna Wait *Guide* p. 114 Mary and Joseph Wait *Guide* p. 115	*Alive-O 2* T1L13/14 Preparing *Guide* p. 155 Preparing for the Birth of Jesus *Guide* p. 156

4. Christmas	*Alive-O 3* T1L15 The Moment They'd All Been Waiting For *Guide* p. 29	*Alive-O 4* T1L14 Jesus – A Light For All *Guide* p. 70	*Alive-O* T1L15 Jesus is Born *Guide* p. 116	*Alive-O 2* T1L15 Celebrating the Birth of Jesus *Guide* p. 157
5. Special Places/ Lent	*Alive-O* T2L7 A Place to Celebrate *Guide* p. 36 *Alive-O 3* T2L4 Lent – Turning Time *Guide* p. 36	*Alive-O 2* T2L6 Special Places *Guide* p. 79	*Alive-O* T2L7 A Place to Celebrate *Guide* p. 121 *Alive-O 3* T2L4 Lent – Turning Time *Guide* p. 121	*Alive-O 4* T2L4 Lent – Reconnecting *Guide* p. 164
6. Easter	*Alive-O* T2L9 Easter *Guide* p. 42 *Alive-O 3* T2L10 A Time for Joy *Guide* p. 42	*Alive-O 2* T2L10 Easter *Guide* p. 83 *Alive-O 4* T2L9 The Passion and Death of Jesus *Guide* p. 83	*Alive-O 3* T2L9 A Time for Joy *Guide* p. 128	*Alive-O 4* T2L9 The Passion and Death of Jesus *Guide* p. 169 T2L10 The Resurrection *Guide* p. 170
7. Mary	*Alive-O 3* T3L1 Mary's Joy *Guide* p. 43	_____	*Alive-O 3* T3L1 Mary's Joy *Guide* p. 129	*Alive-O 4* T3L1 Mary Our Mother *Guide* p. 171
8. End of school year celebration	*Alive-O 3* T3L8 Time to Go – Alive-O! *Guide* p. 51	*Alive-O 2* T3L7 Alive-O! *Guide* p. 92	*Alive-O* T3L7 Alive-O! *Guide* p. 137	*Alive-O 4* T3L11 Time to Go – Alive-O! *Guide* p. 181

In summary, the following reminders might be useful when planning your school visit:
- Decide on your time allocation.
- Review the options available to you in terms of theme/season.
- Choose a theme/lesson.
- Read the background to the lesson in the teacher's manual.
- Read the objectives for the lesson ('What am I trying to do?' and 'Why?').
- Read through the different lesson elements: Song, Story, Chatting, Art, Video, Prayertime.
- Decide which element(s) you will concentrate on during this particular visit.
- Make a brief note of what it is you intend to do/say.

Section Two: *Alive-O* Through the Liturgical Year

Theme 1: Beginning the new school year
Time of Visit: Early to Mid September

Scope: All Classes

Alive-O, Alive-O 2, Alive-O 3 and Alive-O 4 each begin the year by getting the children to reflect on what it means to start a brand new school year. The school day offers the children an opportunity to engage with others in learning and fun. Within this structured environment the children can develop an understanding of what it means to belong to a group/community. They can explore their independence from home, develop a sense of their own identity and come to know what it feels like to be connected to themselves, to others, to the wider world and, ultimately, to God.

The beginning of the year might be an opportune time to visit the classes. An initial visit to Junior Infants (Primary One) will help the younger children become familiar with the 'outside' visitor, while Senior Infants, First and Second Class (Primary Two, Three and Four) will be delighted to welcome back an old friend.

Note: *All page references to the* Alive-O *programme refer to the teacher's manuals, unless otherwise stated.*

Junior Infants/Primary One:
Settling In: Term 1, Lesson 3 (*Alive-O*, p. 15)

What am I trying to do?
To help the children to feel more at ease in the school setting.

Why?
So that having experienced the feelings of security and care, they will be better able to engage in the activities of the school and, more particularly, in the learning process.
Consequently, they will be able to appreciate God's love and care more fully.

For your visit choose from the following lesson elements and suggestions:

Song
Invite the children to sing *I have a name* (Term 1, Lesson 2). You could join in the simple activity that accompanies this song by introducing yourself to the class and inviting them to introduce themselves to you.

Alternatively, they might like to sing one of the other songs that accompany this lesson: *At Home In School* or *Monday Morning*.

Story
Read or invite the children to tell the story *Miriam and Moses and Mum*.

Miriam and Moses and Mum

Miriam was very happy and Miriam was very sad. She was happy because she had a new little baby brother. She was very sad because her mammy said they would not be able to keep him. The king didn't allow Miriam's people to keep their baby boys. Miriam cried. Miriam's mammy cried and the baby cried too.

Then Miriam stopped crying. She got cross. 'We will just have to DO something,' she said to her mammy.

'You are right, Miriam,' her mammy replied. 'We do not want our baby to go away from us. We must make a plan.' And that is what they did.

Miriam and her mammy made a special basket to keep the baby safe and warm. Then they wrapped him in a blanket and laid him in the basket because they could not keep him in their own house with them. They took the baby to the river Nile and they hid him in his basket among the tall rushes where no one would find him.

Then Miriam's mammy told her to hide nearby and keep watch over her little brother.

Now it was a very hot day and after a short time the king's daughter and her servants came to swim in the river. The princess spotted the basket in the rushes and sent one of her servants to see what was in it and to bring it to her.

Poor Miriam watched from her hiding place. She didn't know what to do.

The princess looked into the basket and saw the baby. She knew he was one of the babies that her father, the king, did not allow. But he was crying and she felt sorry for him. 'I must find someone to look after him for me,' she said.

Just then Miriam jumped out of the bushes and ran to the princess, shouting, 'My mammy is very good at minding babies, I could go and get her for you if you like.'

'Very well,' said the princess. 'But I must give him a name first. I will call him Moses because I pulled him out of the water.' Then the princess told Miriam's mammy to take the baby home and look after and feed him until he was a bit bigger. She gave her some money for minding him.

Miriam and her mammy were very happy. They had to let the baby go, but he had come back to them again. 'Phew! Thank God,' they said together.

Chatting

Chatting about coming to school: What day is it today? Do you know which days of the week you come to school? Do you know which days you stay at home? How do you know when to get up for school? Does someone call you on the days when you're not going to school? What do you do at home before you come to school each day?

What do you like most about being at home? What do you like most about being at school? What do you like to do at school that you can't do at home? What new things have you been doing since you came to school? Can you remember the names of some people you have met since you came to school?

Chatting about the story: Do you think Moses was afraid in the water without his mammy or his sister? How did the sister help him? Do you have a big sister or a little sister? Do you have a big brother or a little brother? Did the baby like going away from his mammy? Do you think he would have been happy when his mammy came to take him home? Do you like leaving home in the morning to come to school?

Pupil Book

Chat to the children about the pictures on page 3. Invite them to identify what the two pictures have in common.

Worksheet/Workbook

The children may have completed the worksheet that accompanies this lesson. You may like to ask to see the completed worksheet and chat to the children about their picture. (Worksheet 3)

Video

Watch the video piece 'Let's Start at the Beginning' with the class. Chat to the children about what they see on the video.

Prayertime

You might like to lead the children in prayer, using the following Prayertime text.

Sign of the Cross

Leader

We light our candle.

We thank God for being with us always.

Thank you, God, for all the people who mind us.
For the people who mind us at home.
For mammies.

All
Thank you, God.

Leader
For daddies.

All
Thank you, God.

Leader
For brothers.

All
Thank you, God.

Leader
For sisters.

All
Thank you, God.

Leader
For grannies.

All
Thank you, God.

Leader
For grandads.

All
Thank you, God.

Leader
Is there someone special who minds you who you would like to thank God for? *(Pause)*

(Children name people at home.)

All
Thank you, God. Amen.

Morning Prayer

Sign of the Cross

Senior Infants/Primary Two:
Getting Along Together: Term 1, Lesson 4 (*Alive-O 2*, p. 23)

What am I trying to do?
To explore the need we have for others, and to affirm the child's capacity for play.

Why?
So that the children will come to a deeper understanding of themselves as interdependent people needing co-operation and support from others, and with the capacity to offer this same support and co-operation to those around them.

For your visit choose from the following lesson elements and suggestions:

Song
Sing or invite the children to sing *One Won't Do*. Chat to them about the song.

Story
Read or invite the children to tell the story *Hey Diddle Diddle*.

Hey Diddle Diddle
Hey Diddle Diddle,
The Cat and the Fiddle,
The Cow jumped over the moon,
The Little Dog laughed
To see such fun,
And the Dish ran away with the Spoon.

And that is where this story begins. When Fiddle saw Dish and Spoon running away, it shouted, 'Stop. Wait for me.'

'And me,' Cat miaowed.
'Me too,' barked Little Dog.
'Us two as well,' said Cow and Moon.

As they ran, Dish and Spoon called out:
'You can't catch us,
You're too slow.
You can't play with us,
Away we go!'
And they ran on and on and on.

The others chased after them up hill and down. But they were not fast enough to catch Dish and Spoon, who ran around the corner and hid behind Little Jack Horner and his plum pie.

After a little while, along came the others. They were huffing and puffing.

'We are trying to catch up with Dish and Spoon,' Cow told Jack Horner. 'They don't want us to play with them because we cannot run very fast.'

Suddenly Dish and Spoon jumped out of the corner and ran off laughing. As they ran they called out:
'You can't catch us,
You're too slow.
You can't play with us,
Away we go!'
And they ran on and on and on.

The others ran after them up hill and down but they could not catch Dish and Spoon.

Dish and Spoon ran to Mother Hubbard's cupboard. The cupboard door was open. They hid inside.

After a little while, along came the others. They huffed and puffed. 'O Mother Hubbard,' squeaked Fiddle, 'we have been running all day to try and catch Dish and Spoon. But they don't want us to play with them because we cannot run very fast. Have you seen them anywhere?'

'Let me have a look in my cupboard,' said kind Mother Hubbard. As soon as she opened the door, Dish and Spoon jumped out of the cupboard and ran off laughing. As they ran they called out:
'You can't catch us,
You're too slow.
You can't play with us,
Away we go!'
And they ran on and on and on.

The others chased after them up hill and down but they could not catch Dish and Spoon.

Then Little Dog barked. 'STOP STOP STOP!' Everyone stopped. They flopped down on the ground. 'This is no fun,' he barked crossly.

'You are right Little Dog,' agreed the others.

'Dish and Spoon can play their game,' said Moon, 'it's no fun for us.'

'I have an idea,' said Mother Hubbard, 'why don't we all play a different game?' And that is exactly what they did. They began to play ring-a-ring-a-rosies together.

'You can't catch us,
You're too slow.
You can't play with us,
Away we go!'

called out Dish and Spoon. But no one chased them. Not Cow or Moon, not Cat or Fiddle, or Little Dog, or any of the others.

'This is no fun,' said Dish to Spoon. Now the others were having all the fun. 'I wonder if they will let us join in their game?' Spoon asked Dish.

What do **you** think?

Chatting
Chatting about the story: Can you remember who was in the story? Which one did you like best? Can you remember some of the places where Dish and Spoon hid? Do you ever play hide-and-seek? What good hiding places do you know? Could you play hide-and-seek by yourself? Why did Dish and Spoon not want the others to play with them? Did you ever feel like that? Do you think it was fair to leave the others out because they couldn't run fast? If you were with Cow, Moon, Fiddle etc. in the story, would you let Dish and Spoon join in your game at the end?

Pupil Book
Chat to the children about the pictures on pages 4 and 5: Can you find all the characters in the 'Hey Diddle Diddle' rhyme? Can you see Old Mother Hubbard? Look at Dish and Spoon as they jump out of the cupboard – they are smiling. Why do you think they are smiling?

Video
Watch the video piece 'Here We Go' with the class. Chat to the children about what they see on the video.

Prayertime
You might like to lead the children in prayer, using the following Prayertime text.

Sign of the Cross

Leader
We light our candle and we remember that God is always with us.
Today we thank God for one of our favourite things in the whole world – play.

For time to play.

All
Thank you, God, we pray.

Leader
For others to play with.

All
Thank you, God, we pray.

Leader
For games.

All
Thank you, God, we pray.

Leader
For things to play with.

All
Thank you, God, we pray.

Leader
For fun.

All
Thank you, God, we pray.

Leader
For our special places to play in.

All
Thank you, God, we pray.

Leader
We pray together:

All
God, our Father, I come to say
Thank you for your love today.
Thank you for my family,
And all the friends you give to me.
Guard me in the dark of night,
And in the morning send your light. Amen.

Sign of the Cross

First Class/Primary Three:
We Belong Together: Term 1, Lesson 5 (*Alive-O 3*, p. 43)

What am I trying to do?
To further explore and celebrate the children's experience of belonging in First Class/Primary Three.

Why?
So that they will be more aware of themselves as belonging to First Class/Primary Three and understand better the sense of identity that goes with the experience of belonging.

For your visit choose from the following lesson elements and suggestions:

Song
Sing or invite the children to sing *Christ is My Light* or *Together Again*. Chat to them about the song.

Chatting
Chatting about the class: Chat to the children about their new class, e.g. Does this class have a name? If you could choose a name for the class, what might you choose? Is your class special in any way? I don't belong to this class so describe your class for me. What sort of class would you like to be? (If the children have made a Class Code, you might like to get them to explain it to you.)

Chatting about belonging to a group: Chat to the class about what it is like to belong to a group, e.g. Have you ever thought about all the people we belong with – at home, at school, in the neighbourhood, in the parish? How do we come to belong to a group? How do we come to belong to a family? to a school? to a parish? to God? What does it mean when we say we belong to a group? What does it mean to enrol in a group? (If the class have made a Class Enrolment Book with all their names, you might like to ask them to show the book to you.)

Pupil Book
Chat to the children about the poem and the pictures on page 6.

Video
Watch the video piece 'Belonging' with the children. Chat to them about what they see and hear.

Prayertime
At the end of this week the children celebrate the fact that they belong to a particular class this year by participating in a special Enrolment Ceremony. You might like to lead the children in this ritual using the following text.

Sign of the Cross

All *(sing)*
Together Again

Leader
Today we celebrate the fact that we are now in a new class and have begun a new year.
We thank God for all the people we belong with.
We belong with our families at home.
We belong with our class at school.
We belong with the followers of Jesus.
Today we celebrate our belonging to this class, this year.
We pray:

All
Blessed be God.

Leader *(calling out each child's name in the order in which they appear in the Enrolment Book)*
_____ *(name)*, what class do you belong to?

Child *(stands and answers)*
I belong to First Class/Primary Three.

If time allows, you might like to ask each child to come forward and sign the Enrolment Book. Or if you are creating the Enrolment Book during the ceremony, invite each child to come forward and to place her/his sheet in the book. This will depend on the preference of the class teacher.

All
Blessed be God.

Leader *(on raising the Enrolment Book)*
God, we know that you are always with us.
We know that you will be with us each day of the new year.
Bless our class as we belong together.
Let's stand, hold hands and sing:

All *(sing)*
Christ is my Light

Sign of the Cross

Second Class/Primary Four:
School Spirit: Term 1, Lesson 3 (*Alive-O 4*, p. 29)

What am I trying to do?
To explore with the children the nature of what connects them to each other in school.

Why?
So that they may begin to develop a sense of connectedness and to experience the spirit within which this connectedness is lived out each day in school.

For your visit choose from the following lesson elements and suggestions:

Song
Sing or invite the children to sing *How Lucky We Are!* Chat to them about the song.

Story
Read or invite the children to tell the story *The Beehive*.

The Beehive
Fiona's bee did not come back. She had work to do. You see, Fiona's bee was a worker bee. While she was still very young she cleaned and polished the cells that the new little bees would be born from. Later, when she was bigger, she learned how to produce wax and shape it into a honeycomb for storing honey. Finally, when the little pollen-baskets on her legs were fully grown she flew off every day to search the flowers for pollen and nectar, which she carried back in her baskets to the hive.

While she worked, she also danced. All worker bees must know how to dance. Fiona's bee learned a special dance which she danced to show other worker bees where she had found her pollen so that they could go there too.

Fiona's bee was a very busy little worker. She worked so hard that she didn't have time to come back to Fiona. Although Fiona had been afraid that she or Old Mrs Williams might get stung, the little bee had just one sting which was only to be used in an emergency – as a last resort, if something or someone blocked her path back to the hive. But Fiona and Old Mrs Williams had not blocked her path; fortunately they had helped her back to her hive.

Sometimes in the summer the hive would become very hot. Then Fiona's bee would use her wings to fan the very important Queen bee and cool her down. Every hive has a Queen bee who is bigger than all the others and who lays eggs which, with the help of male bees called drones, hatch out into new bees.

At the end of the summer Fiona's bee and the other workers take a well-earned rest for the winter. They hibernate in their hive where all the bees enjoy sharing the honey they worked so hard to store up.

One day Old Mrs Williams came round to Fiona's house. 'I have a present for you,' she said, smiling, as she handed Fiona a delicious pot of golden honey.

'Where did you get that?' Fiona asked.

'A little bee gave it to me,' the old woman laughed.

Chatting
Chatting about the story: What happens in a beehive? What does honey look like? A beehive is a very busy place – can you remember some of the jobs that have to be done? What kind of work must be done in a school so that everyone can grow and learn? Does everybody do the same job? Name some of the jobs that people in school do every day? What work do you do? What would happen if all the work got mixed up? Do you think that people in school co-operate with one another? Where do you see this happening? What would the school be like if people didn't co-operate with one another?

Pupil Book
Chat to the children about the picture on page 3.

Video
Watch the video piece 'School Spirit' with the class. Chat to the children about what they see and hear on the video.

Prayertime
The children in Second Class/Primary Four will be making their First Communion/First Penance later in the school year. You might like to lead the children in an Enrolment Ceremony to mark the beginning of their preparation for the sacraments. Preparation for this ceremony needs to be done in consultation with the class teacher.

Note: This celebration marks a stage in the process of the children's initiation into membership of the Church. Integrating the following celebration into the Vigil Mass or Sunday Mass might be worth considering.

The lighted paschal candle should be placed in the sanctuary area before the ceremony begins.

All *(sing)*
Connected

Entrance Procession: *Children form a procession, each carrying their baptismal candle (unlit). A child/children carries the Enrolment Certificates. When the children reach the top of the church they bow, then return to join their parents/guardians or*

accompanying adults in their seats. The child/children carrying the Enrolment
Certificates go to the altar where the priest receives the certificates. Children bow,
then return to join the parents or guardians, who will have their baptismal candles.

The priest welcomes the children, their parents/guardians, and the teacher(s).

Welcome
Priest
God our Father, we know that you love us as a mother loves her child. We
know that you care for us as a father cares for his child. Today we come
together to ask you to bless the children of Second Class/Primary Four, as
they prepare for their First Penance and First Communion.

Liturgy of the Word
Priest
The Lord be with you.

All
And also with you.

Priest
A reading from the holy Gospel according to Mark.

More and more people came to see Jesus. Everyone wanted to speak to him
face to face. They wanted to tell him all their worries and troubles. They
wanted to tell him about the good things that were happening to them. They
waited for hours to get near him. It took a long time to get close to Jesus
because Jesus listened carefully to each person's story. Then he gave each one
his blessing. The crowds got bigger and bigger. The line of waiting people
grew longer and longer. 'How strong he is,' thought the apostles. 'He can
stand for hours meeting people and listening to them. Does he ever get
tired?'

As the sun was beginning to set, a group of grown-ups and their children
came over the hill towards Jesus. 'We have come to see Jesus,' they said, 'We
want him to bless our children.' But the apostles said, 'No, it is too late. It's
impossible. Jesus is tired. You must go home. He can't see you.'

The people pleaded with the apostles, 'But we want Jesus to bless our
children. We have come a long way.'

Still the apostles said no. 'It's getting dark,' they said, 'Jesus has been here
talking to people and blessing them all day long. There is no time for anyone
else. Go home and come back another day.'

Just then, Jesus saw what was happening. 'Let the children come to me.
Don't stop them,' he said. 'God loves children in a very special way.' So the
children were brought to Jesus and Jesus talked to them and listened to them.
He took the younger ones in his arms. He laid his hands on them and he

blessed them. They knew that he loved them and they felt very happy. That evening they thanked God for Jesus.

Homily

Rite of Renewal of Baptismal Commitment
Priest
We invite the parents/guardians to come forward and light their child's baptismal candle.

Parents/guardians return to their seats and together with the child they hold the baptismal candle.

Priest
As these children prepare to celebrate their First Penance and First Communion we remember the day you first brought them to the church to be baptised. Today we ask you to be with your child with support and love as she/he prepares for First Penance and First Communion.

I invite the adults to stand up.

Do you believe in God the Father?

All
We do.

Priest
Do you believe in Jesus Christ?

All
We do.

Priest
Do you believe in the Holy Spirit?

All
We do.

Priest
Do you promise to love and support these children as they prepare to celebrate First Penance and First Communion?

All
We do.

Priest
As you do, may the love of God the Father support you; may the light of Jesus Christ, the Son of God, guide you; may the Holy Spirit strengthen you.

All
Amen.

Priest

I now invite the children to stand and to help hold their baptismal candles. As you look forward to your First Penance and First Communion, do you promise to work with your teachers and all the people who love you at home, to learn about Jesus and his love for God the Father and for all of us?

All

We do.

Priest

May God the Father, Son and Holy Spirit bless you and may you know God's love in your hearts and learn to share it with others.

All

Amen.

Rite of Enrolment
Priest

Parents/guardians, as the name of your child is called, come forward and present her/him as a candidate for First Penance and First Communion.

We welcome _____ *(name of child)* as he/she enrols for First Penance and First Communion. We ask you to support him/her during the coming year.

Child receives an Enrolment Certificate and returns to her/his seat with her/his parents/guardians.

Round of applause.

Prayers of the Faithful
Priest

The Lord be with you.

All

And also with you.

Priest

For all the children of the parish who are preparing for First Penance and First Communion. We pray to the Lord.

All

Lord, hear our prayer.

Child

For everyone in our class. We pray to the Lord.

All

Lord, hear our prayer.

Child
For all the people who love us at home as they help us to prepare. We pray to the Lord.

All
Lord, hear our prayer.

Child
For the teachers in our school. We pray to the Lord.

All
Lord, hear our prayer.

Priest
For the people in our community. We pray to the Lord.

All
Lord, hear our prayer.

Invite a parent/guardian to read the reflection on p. 433 of Alive-O 4.

Blessing
Priest
May God bless us and keep us.

All
Amen.

Priest
May we know the presence of God, the Father, Son and Holy Spirit, in our hearts, in our lives, in our school and in our community at this special time in the life of our parish.

All
Amen.

Sing: Time and Time and Time Again.
Praise God, praise God.

Sign of the Cross

Theme 2: Hallowe'en/November:
Feast of All Saints and All Souls
Time of visit: Early November

Scope: All Classes

Traditionally November is the month when we remember the dead. It is a time to recall past events and people who shared our lives. Each year from Junior Infants/Primary One to Second Class/Primary Four the children are encouraged to remember those who have gone before us marked with the sign of faith. The theme is approached differently in each year, taking into account the stage of development and sensitivity of young children.

For pupils and teachers alike November can be a very special time to receive a visit from the priest. It offers an appropriate opportunity to reflect with them about people they may know who have died and are now with God. In exploring this theme one needs to be sensitive to the children and to their capacity to fully understand death. Prior to your visit you might like to check with the teacher to ensure that no child in the class has been recently bereaved.

Junior Infants/Primary One:
Hallowe'en: Term 1, Lesson 8 (*Alive-O*, p. 52)

What am I trying to do?
To introduce the children to story-telling, which is an integral part of our religious heritage.

Why?
To encourage the children's natural love of stories, to deepen their appreciation of story-telling as an important form of communication and to link story-telling with our Christian tradition.

For your visit choose from the following lesson elements and suggestions:

Song
Sing or invite the children to sing *Quiet and Still*. Chat to them about the song.

Story
Read or invite the children to tell the story *Granny's Chair* or *Saint Vincent de Paul*.

Granny's Chair
Once upon a time there was a little girl called Báinín who lived with her

granny in a little house on the edge of a big forest. They were very poor. They had no furniture in the house except for a little stool which Granny used for spinning and one big wooden armchair with a big soft red cushion. They had one hen and a cat and a cow. Every day the hen laid two eggs, one for Báinín and one for her granny. Every day Granny would sit at her spinning wheel and spin fine yarn for making warm blankets and warm clothes for the winter.

In the evening Báinín would light the fire and when the flames were crackling up the chimney her granny would sit in the big wooden armchair with the big soft red cushion and tell her a story.

Báinín loved her granny's stories and every evening she would sit beside the hearth and take the black cat up on her knee and stroke him gently while she listened to the story. Báinín was very happy.

'How come you know so many stories, Granny?' Báinín asked one evening as she was lighting the fire.

Granny smiled. 'Ask the cat... ask the cow... ask the hen... they'll tell you how,' she said smiling. That evening she told Báinín a wonderful story about a magic cow that gave magic milk. You only had to milk her the right way and when you poured her milk into a jug, the jug would never be empty.

Next evening, as she was starting to light the fire, Báinín said to her granny, 'How come you know so many wonderful stories, Granny?'

Granny smiled to herself. 'Ask the cat... ask the cow... ask the hen... they'll tell you how,' she said, smiling. That evening Granny told her a wonderful story about a hen who laid golden eggs. You had only to say the right words and the hen would lay one golden egg every day of the week.

Next evening as she was starting to light the fire, Báinín said to her granny, 'How come you know so many wonderful stories, Granny?'

Granny smiled to herself and said, 'Ask the cat... ask the cow... ask the hen... they'll tell you how,' and she smiled again. This time the story was about a cat with magic eyes that could see into the future. You had only to stroke him the right way and his eyes would shine like diamonds and he would look into the future and tell you what would happen. By the time her granny had finished telling the story, Báinín was fast asleep.

The next morning Granny had to go to the market. 'It will soon be winter,' she said, 'and we need to buy food. I may be gone for quite a long time, but do not worry. The cow will give you milk, the hens will lay you eggs and the cat will keep you company.'

'But, Granny,' cried Báinín, 'how will I get a story if you are not here?'

Granny smiled and said, 'Ask the cat... ask the cow... ask the hen... they'll tell you how,' and off she went.

Báinín was lonely when her granny went away. 'If I was like my granny,' she thought, 'I could tell myself a story and I wouldn't be lonely.' No sooner had she said these words than the hen stretched her neck, stood up on her toes, spread out her wings and said in a clucking voice, 'Go to the cow... go to the cat... they'll tell you where the stories are at.'

The black cat stood on his toes, arched his back, swished his tail and said in a miaowing kind of voice, 'Sit on the cushion... sit in the chair... open your mouth... the stories are there!'

Báinín got up from the hearth and went over to her granny's chair. She climbed up on the big wooden chair and sat on the big soft red cushion. She opened her mouth and... out came a story! It was a truly wonderful story. It was a story Báinín had never heard before. 'If only my granny were here now,' said Báinín, 'I could tell her my wonderful story.'

Just then, the cat's eyes glowed like diamonds and he looked at the cottage door and said in a miaowing kind of voice, 'I see her coming... Granny is near... she's opening the door... Granny is here.'

And indeed the cat was right. 'Granny, Granny,' the little girl shouted. She ran to her and threw her arms around her. 'Granny, Granny,' she said, 'I can tell stories, I can tell stories. I must tell you my story about the magic story chair.' And that is exactly what she did.

Saint Vincent de Paul
Vincent de Paul was the name of a little French boy who was born into a poor farm-family more than four hundred years ago. His father helped him through school and was very pleased when he became a priest. He was captured by pirates while on a sea-journey and sold as a slave in North Africa. The people who bought him made him run and show how strong and active he was, just as if they were buying a horse. After a lot of suffering he escaped in a small boat across the sea and at last got back to Paris.

For a long time he felt very sad and felt that God had forgotten him, so he promised that he would spend all the rest of his life helping the poor and miserable people. Why did he do this? Because he told himself that God said that the proper way to show that we love God is to show love for people who are poor and sad. After Vincent did this, he no longer felt sad and miserable.

There were a lot of wars in those years and many people were very miserable with no one to help them; so Vincent got a lot of his friends to promise that they would help him. Some of these people were priests and others were nuns. Vincent used to say that it was not enough to help people who were poor or sick, that you must also show people how to know all about God and how to love God.

Perhaps the most wonderful thing he did was to show ordinary people that they could come together in small groups and show people like themselves the love of Jesus by helping the people in need of help.

He never thought of himself but always of others. If ever anyone needed help for someone, they always thought to ask Vincent first. He wrote thousands of letters to advise people and help them when he could not go to see them, because his health was not good, probably because he was badly treated when he was a slave. He once took the place of a prisoner who was chained to a bench as a galley-slave.

Years after his death, the Pope made him a saint. Lots of people in France visit the museum to see his statue.

If we want to pray to a saint to help people who are sick or in trouble, we can pray to Saint Vincent.

Chatting
Chatting about the story and story-telling: Does anyone tell stories in your home? Does anyone ever read stories to you? What is your favourite story? If someone said 'tell me a story', what story would you tell? What did you like about the story *Granny's Chair/Saint Vincent de Paul?*

Chatting about the Art: If the children have drawn a picture of Vincent de Paul you might like to invite them to talk about their drawings. Alternatively, you could ask them to draw a picture of Saint Vincent de Paul for you.

Pupil Book
Chat to the children about the picture on page 8.

Prayertime
You might like to lead the children in prayer centred on the litany of saints, using the following Prayertime text.

Sign of the Cross

Light candle as usual.

Leader
The saints are remembered all around us in the world.

There are many things called after the saints.

Our church is Saint .... Church. Our school is called after Saint ....

We are all part of God's family with the saints in heaven.

Today we are going to ask the saints to pray for us.

Saint Brigid.

All
Pray for us.

Leader
Saint Patrick.

All
Pray for us.

Leader
Saint Kevin.

All
Pray for us.

Leader
Saint Margaret.

All
Pray for us.

Leader
Saint Columba (Colmcille).

All
Pray for us.

Leader
Saint Thérèse.

All
Pray for us.

Leader
Saint Andrew.

All
Pray for us.

Leader
Saint Joseph.

All
Pray for us.

Leader
Saint Anne.

All
Pray for us.

You can add saints as you think appropriate. They might be linked with the area or with the children in the class.

Glory be to the Father,
And to the Son,
And to the Holy Spirit.

Sign of the Cross

Senior Infants/Primary Two:
Let's Remember: Term 1, Lesson 7 (*Alive-O 2*, p. 58)

What am I trying to do?
To provide an opportunity for the children to remember and pray for those who have died.

Why?
So that the children will have some background upon which they can build an understanding of the concept of the Communion of Saints.

For your visit choose from the following lesson elements and suggestions:

Song
Sing or invite the children to sing *Remember them*. Chat to them about the song.

Story
Read or invite the children to tell the story *The Daffodils*.

The Daffodils
The happy, yellow daffodils stood up straight and tall and smiled their sunniest smile. They wanted every customer who came to the flower stall to notice how fresh and pretty and pleasant they were. 'Someone is sure to buy us soon,' they whispered in each other's petals.

A man and woman came to the stall. 'We would like to buy some flowers for our friend who is in hospital,' they told the stallkeeper. The daffodils smiled as hard as they could. 'She loves red roses,' the woman said. 'Could we have a bunch of red roses please?'

'Certainly,' replied the stallkeeper. The daffodils were very disappointed.

Next, a woman and her daughter came to the stall. They looked around at all the flowers. 'I am getting married,' the girl said, 'and I want some flowers for my bouquet.' The daffodils smiled their sunniest smile. 'I love lillies,' said the girl. 'Could I have some lillies please?'

'Certainly,' replied the stallkeeper. The daffodils were very disappointed.

A man came to the stall. 'I want to say thank you to a special person,' he said, 'so I thought I would buy some flowers for my friend.' The daffodils stood up tall and straight and proud. 'What kind of flowers do you think I should choose?' he asked the stallkeeper.

'We have some lovely daffodils,' she replied. The daffodils smiled and nodded in the breeze.

'What is that beautiful smell?' the man asked, sniffing here and there.

'That must be the chrysanthemums,' said the stallkeeper.

'Then I will take a bunch of those,' said the man.

'Certainly,' said the stallkeeper. The daffodils were very disappointed.

By now the buckets on the stall were almost empty. Soon it would be time for the stallkeeper to pack up and go home. The poor daffodils had lost their sunny smile. They thought no one liked them; no one wanted to buy them. Oh dear! Just then a little boy and his granny came to the stall. 'We want to buy some flowers to put on Grandad's grave,' the little boy explained. 'It is his anniversary tomorrow,' said the granny. 'That was the day he died on last year.'

'Granny, Granny, look at these – these were Grandad's favourite flowers. We must get a big bunch of these,' said the little boy excitedly. The drooping daffodils looked around to see which flowers the boy was pointing to.

'Why, yes, of course,' said Granny. 'Grandad loved daffodils.'

Daffodils! The daffodils could hardly believe it. They stood up straight and fresh again. They smiled their sunny, yellow smile as the stallkeeper lifted them out of their bucket and wrapped a piece of colourful paper around them. Their heads nodded proudly as the little boy carried them off to his grandad's grave.

Chatting

Chatting about the story: Have you ever been in a flower shop? Do you know the names of any flowers? What is your favourite flower? If you had gone to the flower stall in the story, what flower would you have chosen? Did you ever see someone put flowers on a grave? Have you ever put flowers on a grave? Can you remember what kind of flowers they were? What colour were they? Tell us about the person who was dead.

Chatting about the wider family: As well as the people we live with every day, we are part of a bigger family. These people are our relations and they don't usually live in the same house as us. Can you tell me about your relations? (Talk to the children about cousins, aunts, uncles, grandparents, etc.) Perhaps one of your relations is dead. Do you remember them? Tell us about them. Do you know any stories about them?

Chatting about the wider community: Everybody lives in a community where they have neighbours and friends. Tell us about the people who live around you. When do you see them? Can you remember a time when your neighbours helped you or someone in your home? What happened? Can you think of a time when you or someone at home did something kind for a neighbour? Tell us about it. Friends and neighbours help one another.

Friends and neighbours feel sad when someone dies. When someone we know dies, we can pray for them and ask God to care for them.

Prayertime
You might like to lead the children in prayer for those who have died, using the following Prayertime text.

Sign of the Cross

Leader
We light our candle. It reminds us of God's love and care for each one of us at all times. God is with us right now. God is always close by, always taking special care of us.

Today we ask God to look after all those who have died.

We remember all the grans and grandads who have died.

All
May they rest in peace. Amen.

Leader
We remember all the mams and dads who have died.

All
May they rest in peace. Amen.

Leader
We remember all those who used to live with us who have died.

All
May they rest in peace. Amen.

Leader
We remember all the neighbours who have died.

All
May they rest in peace. Amen.

(Encourage those children who wish to do so, to name someone they know who has died and for whom they wish to pray. The other children can respond by praying: 'May he/she/they rest in peace. Amen'.)

Leader
We pray together:

All
God, bless them and keep them,
May they rest in peace. Amen.

Sign of the Cross

First Class/Primary Three:
We Remember Together: Term 1, Lesson 6 (*Alive-O 3*, p. 55)

What am I trying to do?
To help the children to reflect on their own experience of remembering and to provide them with an opportunity during the month of November to remember those who have died.

Why?
So that the children may begin to be aware of the importance of remembering those who have died and be able to link this month with the liturgical year, the Feast of All Souls and the Feast of All Saints.

For your visit choose from the following lesson elements and suggestions:

Song
Sing or invite the children to sing *Columba* or *Remember Them*. Chat to the children about the song.

Story
Read or invite the children to tell the story *Columba*.

Columba
Most stories begin with beginnings,
    This story begins with the end
Of an old man's life on an island
    And a horse's goodbye to his friend.

One Saturday morning Columba
    Woke up in bed and just knew
That this, the last day of the week,
    Was going to be his last day too.

He jumped out of bed, determined,
    It being the day that was in it,
To continue his life as he had always done,
    Living, to the very last minute.

Resting his head in his hands he prayed,
    [1]'Buíochas le Dia go deo!
Molaimid thú, móraimid thú
    Thall 's abhus 's anseo.'

Patting the pillow, 'Goodbye Bed,' he said,
    'In you I have known rest 'n peace,
No matter how dark or dreary the night
    You cradled me, *[2]'rís 's arís.*

Goodbye Window,' he said, opening it wide,
  'You brought fresh air and light to my life.
You helped me breathe; you helped me see
  Through troubles and struggles and strife.

Goodbye Room,' he said, as he closed the door,
  'You gave me space – just to *be*
On my own, with you, when I needed –
  Just the two of us; you Room, and me.'

Neither Bed, Window nor Room
  Moved or uttered a word,
But the old saint knew, as old saints do,
  That each one had listened and heard.

It was May, the first month of summer,
  Columba's last of the year.
His friends were at work in the western fields,
  They stopped as the old man drew near.

'I have this notion,' Columba said,
  'Don't ask me how, what or why,
But I know in my heart, I feel in my bones,
  It's time, time for goodbye.'

'Where are you going?' they asked in alarm.
  'I'm going away,' he replied,
'I won't be back, but I'll see you again,
  If you know what I mean,' he smiled.

That said, he opened the doors of the barn
  And blessed its stores of grain.
*³'*Tá Dia maith*, you'll not want for food
  When I'm gone,' he repeated again.

Tired, though not yet quite finished,
  Columba sat down for a rest
On an old millstone by the side of the road.
  'Brother Diarmuid,' he said, 'Have you guessed?'

'Guessed what, Brother?' Diarmuid his friend asked,
  'I feel cross, yet I'm sad deep inside.
You talk of goodbye, of going away.
  What is it you're trying to hide?'

Just at that moment a *⁴*sean-chapall bán*
  With head drooping low in dismay,
Plodded along towards Columba, and stood
  Bereft of a whinney, or neigh.

49

Silent, he stood there, his mild mannered eyes
  Filled with sorrow intense.
He knew his old friend was going to die,
  Though how he knew – that baffles sense!

'Goodbye my sean-chapall,' Columba said,
  'Surefooted, dependable friend.
On the broad of your back you carried me,
  *⁵Beannacht Dé leat. Amen.'

He stroked the old horse's forehead,
  Its eyes filled with tears to the brim.
They spilled over, rolled down its cheeks,
  And dropped from its quivering chin.

'Your tears are upsetting Columba,
  Go away horse,' Diarmuid protested.
'Let him be!' said Columba, 'this dumb creature knew,
  Though you have not even guessed it.

He senses that I am dying.
  I tell you, else you wouldn't know,
This creature's natural horse-sense
  Is a wonder God has bestowed.'

A last look to Ireland, then back to Iona,
  Where he had come to reside.
As the sean-chapall turned and ambled away,
  Columba lay down – and died.

Columba just lay down and died
  At rest in peace. Amen.
Now this story has reached its beginning
  Because death is never the end.

*¹	Glory to God above.	*³	God is good
	We praise you. We bless you, we thank you.	*⁴	Old White Horse
	We live out each day in your love.	*⁵	God bless you
*²	Again and again		

Chatting

Chatting about remembering: Close your eyes and see what you can remember about yesterday. Is it easy to remember? What kind of things are really easy to remember? What kind of things are difficult to remember? Can you remember when you were a small child? Can you remember what you learnt yesterday, last week, last month? What would happen if we couldn't remember at all?

Chatting about those who have died: The story of Columba tells us about the day he died. How do you think he felt that day? How did his friends feel? Perhaps someone you know has died. Tell us about them. Do you remember them? Does your family remember them in any way? Do you think that Columba's friend remembered him? Does the story help us to remember Columba? Do you know stories about anyone who has died? What would happen if we didn't tell stories about people who have died?

Pupil Book
Chat to the children about the picture on page 7. Talk to them about what they see in the picture.

Art
In this lesson the children have an option of making a story cross. This cross is a reminder to them of someone who has died. You might like to chat to the children about the crosses if they have been or are in the process of being made.

Video
Watch the video piece 'November' with the children. Chat to them about what they hear and see.

Prayertime
You might like to lead the children in prayer around their story crosses, using the following Prayertime text.

Sign of the Cross

Leader *(as the candle is lit)*
God the light of yesterday.
God the light of today.
God the light of tomorrow.

Today we are going to remember those who have died.

All *(sing)*
Remember Them

Invite the children to come forward.

All *(after each group of children)*
Eternal rest grant unto them, O Lord.
May they rest in peace. Amen.

Leader
We remember those who are feeling sad and lonely because someone they love has died. We ask God to remember all those who have died. Eternal rest grant unto them, O Lord.

All
May they rest in peace. Amen.

Sign of the Cross

Second Class/Primary Four:
The Feast of All Saints: Term 1, Lesson 6 (*Alive-O 4*, p. 66)

What am I trying to do?
To help the children to explore the spirit and significance of the ordinary events of their lives.

Why?
So that the children's celebration and understanding of the Feast of All Saints on 1 November may be enhanced and deepened.

For your visit choose from the following lesson elements and suggestions:

Song
Sing or invite the children to sing *Sanctus*. Chat to them about the song.

Story
Read or invite the children to tell the story *Mary Mary's Garden*.

Mary Mary's Garden
Have you ever heard the rhyme:

> Mary, Mary, quite contrary
> How does your garden grow?
> With Silver Bells and Cockle Shells
> And Pretty Maids all in a row.

Mary Mary was indeed quite contrary, but no one could blame her for that. People talked as though there was nothing in her garden but Silver Bells and Cockle Shells and Pretty Maids all in rows. This irritated Mary Mary. One day she talked to her flowers: 'You are all so wonderful and so different; it's a pity people have such narrow ideas about our garden.'

Then Mary Mary had an idea. 'I know,' she cried, 'let's have an Open Day, then everyone can come and see how wide and varied our garden is.'

Mary Mary made some posters announcing the Open Day. People queued to see inside the famous garden.

'This way please,' said Mary Mary, leading them round. Naturally, the first things they admired were the Silver Bells and Cockle Shells and neat rows of Pretty Maids.

'So neat, so orderly, so tidy,' they said, smiling.

'This way please,' Mary Mary said, leading them further into the garden.

'Such rare Roses,' the people commented, looking to the left.
'Such lavish Lillies,' they said, looking to the right.
'Such delightful Delphiniums,' they said, looking all around.

53

'You have a truly wonderful garden, Mary Mary, so full of exceptional flowers, each one a perfect example of its kind,' they congratulated her.

'This way please,' said Mary Mary, smiling to herself as she led them to the heart of the garden.

'Oh dear!' the people gasped in shock. Before them lay a chaotic mass of wild flowers, growing here, there and everywhere. 'What went wrong?' they asked Mary Mary. 'We wouldn't expect to see a sight like this in a garden such as *yours.*'

'Nothing is wrong,' Mary Mary smiled. 'There is room in my garden for every kind of living thing. These wild flowers have such a generous spirit. They grow to be the very best Buttercups and Daisies and Primroses they can be. No one could ask more of them. They are the very heart of my garden.'

'But Cowslips, common Honeysuckle, Clover…,' the people exclaimed, pointing in dismay. 'These are not proper garden flowers.'

'Cowslips are delightful; such beautiful yellow bells. No one has bells quite like the Cowslip. And the Honeysuckle…just smell it…,' Mary Mary said, sniffing the scent deep into her nostrils. 'There is no scent like the scent of the Honeysuckle. And Clover – such a brave little plant. It will grow where no other plant will grow.'

'Well, you have indeed surprised us, Mary Mary, you have given us all something to think about,' the people said, shaking her hand as they left the garden.

'And here is something else for you to think about,' Mary Mary said,

> I'm Mary Mary and quite contrary
> To how the nursery rhyme goes.
> My garden has all kinds of flowers and plants
> Most of which *don't* grow in rows.
>
> Each one of them grows in its own quiet way
> To become one of life's little pleasures.
> Though they bud and bloom and then die away
> Their beauty gives joy beyond measure!

Chatting

Chatting about the story: What is your favourite flower? Why were the people surprised to find wild flowers in Mary Mary's garden? How do you think the wild flowers felt as they stood in the garden and saw how the people reacted to them? What words would you use to describe how they felt?

Chatting about saints: Chat to the children about saints. Do you know any saints? Are you called after a saint? Can you remember any stories about saints? What makes a person a saint? Do saints have to be well-known people? Can 'ordinary' people be saints? What about people who have died – can they be saints? Have you ever known anyone, who is dead now, whom you think would have been 'a saint'?

Pupil Book
Chat to the children about the picture and text on page 6.

Art
On day three of this week's lesson the children are invited to make a Garden of Remembrance in commemoration of someone who has died. If the children have completed this work you might like to ask them to talk to you about it.

Video
Watch the video piece 'Feast of All Saints' with the class. Chat to the children about what they see and hear on the video.

Prayertime
You might like to lead the children in a simple ritual in honour of the Feast of All Saints and All Souls, using the following Prayertime text.

Sign of the Cross

Leader
We light our candle.

We know that God is with us today. God was with us yesterday. We know that God will be with us tomorrow. Today as we place our flowers in the Garden of Remembrance we remember those who lived ordinary lives and who have died and are now with God. We remember how they lived as Jesus asked them to. We ask God to care for all those who have died. We pray:

All
Eternal rest grant unto them, O Lord.
May they rest in peace.

The leader invites each child in turn to come forward and to place her/his flower in the garden. As he/she places the flower, invite the child to name the person out loud. As each child names her/his person, the class responds:

All
Eternal rest grant unto her/him, O Lord.
May she/he rest in peace.

Leader
In this month of November we remember all those who have died. We

remember those who are feeling sad and lonely today because someone close to them has died. We ask God to comfort all those who are sad as we pray to Mary.

All
Hail Mary, full of grace,
The Lord is with thee.
Blessed art thou among women
And blessed is the fruit of thy womb, Jesus.
Holy Mary, mother of God,
Pray for us sinners,
Now, and at the hour of our death. Amen.

Sign of the Cross

Theme 3: Advent
Time of Visit: Month of December

Scope: All Classes

The Church sets aside Advent as a time of preparation, waiting and longing for the coming of Jesus Christ. It focuses on the coming of Jesus in history, the coming of Christ into our lives today and, through us, into the world, and looks forward to the coming of Christ at the end of time.

Advent is a time when children can be helped to prepare for the Christmas event. During the Advent season *Alive-O* recalls with the children the significant moments in the infancy narratives. Frequently this is done over a series of lessons. While honouring the centrality of the original biblical stories, *Alive-O* offers different perspectives and approaches in line with the stage of development of children.

Junior Infants/Primary One:
Simeon and Anna Wait: Term 1, Lesson 13 (*Alive-O*, p. 94)

What am I trying to do?
To offer the children an opportunity to explore their experience of waiting and to foster in them the capacity to wait.

Why?
So that they will:
- be able to identify the feelings associated with waiting and cope with their own experience of waiting;
- begin to recognise some of the 'waiting' moments that punctuate their own lives;
- focus more specifically on their present experience of waiting for Christmas.

Mary and Joseph Wait: Term 1, Lesson 14 (*Alive-O*, p. 102)

What am I trying to do?
To help the children to recognise that there are different kinds of waiting; specifically to help them to be aware of the kind of waiting that is hopeful. To introduce children to the story of the journey of Mary and Joseph from Nazareth to Bethlehem.

Why?
So that they will reflect on their own experience of waiting for Christmas.

For your visit choose from the following lesson elements and suggestions:

Song
Sing or invite the children to sing *Waiting* or *Carol of a Journey*. Chat to them about the song.

Story
Read or invite the children to tell one of the Advent stories: *Anna; Simeon; Anna and Simeon; Mary and Joseph Go on a Journey*.

Anna
When Anna was a young girl she was very happy about something.

Anna wasn't quite sure YET what it was she was happy about. She couldn't say exactly, but it didn't matter, she was still very happy. The only thing Anna did know about whatever it was, was that she had to wait for it.

Anna didn't mind waiting. If there was one thing in this world Anna was very good at, it was waiting. She wasn't the tallest girl in her family, she wasn't the fastest runner in the neighbourhood, she wasn't the best singer of all the children, but Anna was better at waiting than everyone else.

Every day and every week and for a whole year, Anna waited. And do you think, after all that time, Anna gave up waiting?

Anna did not give up waiting. Even though she didn't know exactly what she was waiting for, didn't know exactly what it would look like, didn't know exactly when it would come, she was certain that it would be very, very important and she was happy that she had been specially chosen to see it. Anna waited another whole year, and another, and another. Anna waited year after year until she was not a child any more, she was a woman. Anna went to the temple, and while she was waiting she prayed.

Another year went by and another ten years went by and another twenty years went by. Still Anna waited. Still she went to the temple. Still she prayed. Still she believed that there was something very special in store for her.

By this time Anna was an old woman. Her hair was silvery white. Her face was old. And still she waited. But she was a little bit worried.

Anna wasn't worried that the thing she was waiting for wouldn't happen. No. She had no doubt that it would happen. She knew it in her heart. She had a feeling in her bones. She had dreamed about it all her life. She had prayed every single day.

The only reason Anna worried was because she knew she was getting old. She knew that she did not have many years left. And she desperately wanted to see what she had waited all her life for. So, when Anna went to the temple she said a special prayer that God would let her see the very important thing she had waited for before it was time for her to die.

One day Old Anna was in the temple. While she was waiting she prayed the same prayer. She asked God, please, to let her see what she had been waiting for. She knew that she had done everything that God wanted her to do. She had kept watching and waiting. And she knew that God would hear her prayer. As she was praying patiently, the doors of the temple opened. Anna looked up.

Simeon

When Simeon was a young boy he was very happy. The reason why he was very happy was because he knew something good was going to happen to him.

Simeon didn't know exactly what was going to happen, but he was certain that it was going to be something good. He had a feeling about it, he had a hunch, he knew in his heart. He knew he only had to wait and see. And Simeon was happy to wait.

Simeon was well used to waiting. There were lots of times when he had to wait. He had to wait to be grown-up and that had taken a very long time, but there was nothing else he could do but wait.

Every day, while he was waiting for the good thing to happen, Simeon saw that other people around him were very busy. They would hurry to the market to buy food. Then they would hurry home to cook it. Then they would hurry to finish their meal because they were busy and they had lots of work to do. Simeon did his work too, but while he was doing it he was also waiting and watching out for the good thing to happen.

Day in and day out, week in and week out, year in and year out, Simeon waited. As he waited he grew older and older. But he was still as excited as he was the first day because he knew that whatever it was that was going to happen, was going to be wonderful.

'But how will you know when it happens?' one of his friends asked. 'How do you know you will not miss it?'

'I will know,' answered Simeon. 'There is no one who is better than I am at watching and waiting. I will not miss it, how could I miss it? I pray, watch carefully and wait patiently, and for now, that is all that needs to be done.'

Simeon was getting old. His hair and his beard were white as snow. His walking was getting slower and he was a little bit worried because his eyes and his ears were not as sharp as they used to be. Perhaps people were right. Perhaps he would not see the wonderful thing he had waited all his life for. Perhaps he would not hear about it.

One day a thought came into Simeon's head. He listened to that thought.

The thought told him to go to the temple. The thought did not tell him why he should go to the temple, and he did not ask. He just went.

When he arrived at the temple he went inside to pray. He heard another voice praying and he looked around. He saw an old woman. Her name was Anna. She was waiting for something too. Simeon and Anna waited and watched and prayed together.

Simeon and Anna

'How long have you been waiting?' Simeon asked Anna.

'I have been waiting all my life,' she answered.

'Me too,' said Simeon.

Then they stopped talking and each one of them went off to a different part of the temple to pray.

Before long the doors of the temple opened. Anna looked up. Simeon looked up. Simeon and Anna walked towards the doors. Simeon held out his arms. Anna smiled with joy. It had come. God had kept his word. At long, long last their waiting was over.

'Praise to you, Lord,' said Anna.

'Blessed be God forever,' said Simeon and he took the baby in his arms.

And do you know who that very special baby was?

(Allow time for the children to answer.)

It was baby Jesus.

Mary and Joseph go on a Journey

One day a messenger came to the village of Nazareth where Mary and Joseph lived. He told them that everyone had to sign their name in a book. They had to go to the town where they belonged to do this. Joseph and Mary had to go to Bethlehem because that was their home town. Caesar, who was the ruler of the land, could then know how many people lived there. Mary was a little worried when she heard this news. Mary and Joseph were waiting for Mary's new baby to be born. They knew the baby would be born very soon. But they had to do what Caesar wanted. So, next day, they set off with their donkey to make the long journey to Bethlehem.

They travelled for several days. Mary was very tired when they finally reached Bethlehem. They decided that, first of all, they would go and sign their names in Caesar's book, then they would find somewhere to rest for the night. And that is what they did. But, they found it very difficult to get a room for the night. They knocked on lots of doors but no one had any room for them. Many people had come to the city to sign their names in Caesar's book. So all the spare rooms were full up.

Mary was getting very anxious. She knew her baby would come very soon. She needed somewhere, anywhere, to rest. Joseph kept on trying to find a place for them. In the end one innkeeper sent them outside the town to a cave in the hillside. It was a cave that shepherds sometimes used when they needed shelter for themselves and their sheep. Mary and Joseph and the donkey set off to the cave.

Not far away, on a hillside, some shepherds were settling their sheep for the night. Everything was quiet and peaceful when suddenly they heard the sound of voices singing. At first the shepherds didn't know where the singing was coming from. Then one of them pointed to the sky. The others looked up and there among the stars they saw lots and lots of angels. It was the angels who were singing. They were singing praises to God, because something wonderful had just happened. At first the shepherds were afraid. They had spent many nights in the hills, but they had never seen a sight like this before. They didn't know what to do. But the angels sang very sweetly and told them not to be afraid. They told them to leave their sheep and go towards the city of Bethlehem. There, in a cave outside the city, they would find something very wonderful indeed. The shepherds did as the angels told them.

Chatting

Depending on what story(ies) you wish to explore with the children, choose from the following chattings.

Anna and Simeon: What do you think about Anna? Do you think she was foolish to spend all those years waiting? What would you do? What's the longest time you have ever waited for something?

What do you think about Simeon? What do you think Simeon was like? Do you think he ever got tired of waiting? What was it that Anna and Simeon were waiting for all through the long weeks and months and years? Who was the special baby they were waiting for? Right now we are waiting for Christmas and at Christmas we will celebrate the birth of Jesus. Christmas Day is Jesus' birthday. Is it difficult for us to wait for Christmas? Why?

Mary and Joseph: Have you ever put your name in a book? Mary and Joseph had to go on a journey to put their names in Caesar's book. Did you ever go on a long journey? Why do you think Mary and Joseph took a donkey with them? They were tired after their long journey – do you ever feel tired after a long journey? What did the shepherds hear from the sky? Do you know any Christmas song? Will we sing a song? What did the angels say to the shepherds? Do you think they were afraid? Were you ever afraid? Where did the shepherds go? Whom did they see?

Video
You might like to show the children one of the following parts of the video piece 'We Belong': the one based on Lesson 13, which is built around the song *Waiting;* the one based on Lesson 14, which is built around the song *Carol of the Journey.* Chat to the children about what they see and hear on the video.

Prayertime
You might like to lead the children in quiet Advent prayer, using the following Prayertime text.

Sign of the Cross

Light the candle.

Leader
Close your eyes...
Still your hands...
Stop your feet from tapping...
Listen to your heart beat...
Still yourself...

Go into your little inside space... relax... we are waiting for Christmas... Christmas is a very special time... Jesus was born on the first Christmas night... God sent Jesus to show us how much God loves us... all the fun and the decorations and the presents that we enjoy at Christmas are signs of our happiness because we know that God loves us...

While we wait for Christmas we could all do something to show someone at home that we love them... think about it... Who do you want to say 'I love you' to? What can you do to show that person your love? You could give them a hug... you could do something to help them... Make up your mind... don't forget to do whatever you have decided this evening.

Open your eyes...
Stretch...

Together we will say our Christmas prayer.

All
'Thank you, God, for Jesus'
Is the prayer we say.
'Thank you, God, for Jesus'
We pray on Christmas Day.

Sign of the Cross

Senior Infants/Primary Four:
Preparing: Term 1, Lesson 13 (*Alive-O 2*, p. 108)

What am I trying to do?
To help the children to focus on their experience of preparing for Christmas.
To introduce them to the story of Mary and Elizabeth, who prepared for the first Christmas.

Why?
So that they will understand the significance of time spent in preparation, and be aware that they are now preparing to celebrate the birth of Jesus at Christmas.

Preparing for the Birth of Jesus: Term 1, Lesson 14 (*Alive-O 2*, p. 115)

What am I trying to do?
To focus imaginatively on the lead-up to the birth of Jesus.

Why?
So that the children will focus on their present experience of this time of the year as a lead-up to the celebration of the birth of Jesus.

For your visit choose from the following lesson elements and suggestions:

Song
Sing or listen to the children sing *Advent Song* or *Carol of the Journey*. Chat to them about the song.

Story
Read or invite the children to tell one of the following stories: *Two Cousins; The City Prepares; The Shepherds Prepare; The Angels Prepare; The Kings Prepare; Mary and Joseph Prepare.*

Two Cousins
This story is based on Luke 1:39-56 and is adapted for children.

Mary and Elizabeth were cousins. These two cousins had good news: the good news was that Mary and Elizabeth were both going to have new babies! Mary and Elizabeth were very, very happy.

'It is such a pity that my cousin Elizabeth and I live so far apart,' said Mary to herself.

'How I would love to see my cousin Mary, if only we did not live so far apart,' said Elizabeth to herself.

'I shall go on a journey and visit my cousin Elizabeth,' said Mary. 'But it will take a long time to get there. Elizabeth and I have a lot to chat and talk about, so I will stay in her house for many nights. I won't be back for a long time, so I will have to make lots of preparations before I go. Now, let me see, what do I need to take with me? What should I leave behind?'

Mary sat down right then and drew up a list of all the preparations she would have to make. First of all she had to let Elizabeth know she was coming. *How do you think she could do that?*

Second, she had to tell her family and friends that she was going away for a long time.

Third, she had to pack a bag for herself. *What do you think she would need to take with her? Would one bag be enough or should she take two or three? What if the weather should get cold where Elizabeth lived? What if it should rain? What if she should get hungry on the long journey and need something to eat?*

Fourth, Mary wanted to take some presents to Elizabeth. She wondered what Elizabeth might like. *What do you think Elizabeth might like?*

Then Mary had a brilliant idea. 'I know,' she said, 'I will take something for Elizabeth's new baby when it comes.' *What things do you think Mary could take for the new baby Elizabeth was waiting for?*

'Now,' said Mary when she had finished all her preparations, 'I think that is everything, but I'd better go back and check, just in case.'

Let's check all the things Mary had to prepare.
First...
Second...
Third...
Fourth...

Mary was very excited as she went on her journey. Elizabeth was very excited at the news that her cousin Mary was coming to visit.

'Cousin Mary will be staying for many nights,' said Elizabeth to herself, 'and she will be very tired after her long journey. I will have to make some preparations to get the house ready before she comes. Now, let me see, what do I need to do?'

'First, I must tell my husband Zechariah the good news.' 'Zechariah, Zechariah', she called. *Can you remember what Elizabeth has to tell her husband?*

'Second,' said Elizabeth, 'I must get a room ready for Cousin Mary.' *What do you think she would have to do to get a room ready?*

'Third, I must get some food in, and get some baking done,' said Elizabeth. *What food do you think she would need to get? What do you think she could bake?*

'Fourth, I must make myself nice and tidy for my cousin Mary coming,' thought Elizabeth. *What do you think she had to do to make herself tidy?*

'Now, I think that must be everything,' said Elizabeth, as she looked around the house, checking that everything was in its place. 'But I'd better go back and check, just in case.'

Can you help Elizabeth to check that she hasn't forgotten any of her preparations?
First...
Second...
Third...
Fourth...

'Won't cousin Elizabeth be delighted to see me,' said Mary, smiling to herself as she walked along.

Elizabeth could hardly wait for her cousin Mary to arrive. 'It's such a long time since I saw Mary. I wonder what she'll look like now that she's going to have a new baby?' thought Elizabeth, smiling to herself. *What do you think Mary and Elizabeth look like now that they are getting new babies?*

'Oh No! Oh No! Oh No!' gasped Elizabeth. 'I've just remembered, I forgot something, Oh dear me, I don't know if I have enough time left, I'll have to hurry to the market, Oh dear, Oh dear, Oh dear...', and Elizabeth hurried off. *Can you guess what Elizabeth forgot?* But Mary was almost there, she had almost arrived.

Elizabeth hurried as quickly as she could. When she arrived back at the door of her house she saw her cousin Mary coming up the path. She ran to meet her, shouting, 'Mary, Mary, it's so good to see you.'

Mary ran up the path towards Elizabeth. Mary was delighted to see her cousin. 'Elizabeth, Elizabeth, I'm here, hurrah, hurrah!'

The two cousins hugged and kissed and put their arms around each other. Then they went inside. Mary took off her coat and opened the bag she had packed.

'I've brought a present for your new baby when it comes,' said Mary smiling as she handed the present to her cousin.

Elizabeth laughed. 'I almost forgot,' she said to Mary, 'but I've bought a present for your new baby when it comes too!'

The two cousins opened their presents and held them up. The two cousins looked at each other and burst out laughing. They had bought each other the exact same present!

The City Prepares

The following stories are based on Luke 2:1-24 and Matthew 2:1-12 and have been adapted for children.

Rebecca had a feeling that something special was going to happen. She had never seen the city so busy. Cheese-makers were busy making cheeses. Bakers were baking fresh loaves. Farmers were herding their sheep and goats into the market. Merchants were rolling out metres and metres of cloth for selling, and there were Roman soldiers everywhere. Everyone was busy, as if they were preparing for something special. But no one was busier than the innkeepers. With all the extra crowds of people in the city, they were busy preparing rooms and beds and meals.

Rebecca's mother and father were innkeepers. All day long Rebecca had been answering the door as people called to see if they had any rooms for the night. The last time the city had been this busy was on the festival day. 'Are we having another festival?' she asked her mother. 'Is that why there are so many people in the city?'

'No,' her mother replied. 'These people have not come for a festival. They are coming because Caesar ordered them too. And more and more of them will come tomorrow and the next day. Now I am very busy. I have to make rooms ready for them. Some of them have travelled a long way and they will want somewhere to spend the night.'

'Who is Caesar anyway?' asked Rebecca.

'Caesar is our ruler,' her mother answered.

'Why did Caesar order them to come?' she asked. 'Is something special going to happen?'

'Caesar wants to count how many people live in our land,' her mother replied. 'So he has sent soldiers all over the country to tell people they must come and write their names in a special book. Then he will know how many people live in our country.'

'Will I have to put my name in Caesar's special book?' Rebecca asked.

'Your father will put your name in it,' her mother answered. 'Now I must get out my special dishes and plates for the visitors.'

'What visitors?' asked Rebecca, but her mother was too busy preparing the inn to answer any more questions. 'Take these towels upstairs for me,' she said, 'and then I have another job for you to do.'

As Rebecca was going upstairs she was thinking 'a special book, special dishes and plates, visitors – I feel sure something special is going to happen.'

The Shepherds Prepare

Reuben's father was a shepherd. This evening Reuben was out on the hill helping his father with the sheep. Every evening his father and the other shepherds would prepare for the long night ahead. They would begin by gathering all the sheep together with their lambs. Then when all the flock had settled and the evening grew darker, the shepherds would sit down together and talk and tell stories and have something to eat.

'But tonight seems different from all other nights. The sheep are very restless. It is almost as if they are listening to something, as if they hear something in the wind,' Reuben said to his father.

'That could well be,' his father replied. 'Animals can often hear things that people cannot hear.'

The lambs, too, were bleating more than usual. Just as Reuben and the other shepherds had finally gathered the flock together, Reuben noticed that one lamb, the youngest and smallest lamb, was missing. This little lamb was Reuben's pet. He liked to take special care of it, so he ran off after it.

'Come back little lamb,' he shouted. The little lamb said 'Maaa' and kept on going. Soon Reuben caught him and brought him back.

'Stay here little lamb,' he said. He sat down on the ground and held the lamb tightly in his arms.

Around him the shepherds were preparing for the long night ahead. Some were lighting a little fire to keep warm. Some were preparing food to eat. Some were laying out warm blankets to sleep on. Some were counting the sheep to make sure they were all there.

Reuben's little lamb struggled in his arms. He wanted to get away. He wanted to go somewhere. 'What is the matter little lamb?' asked Reuben, stroking him gently. 'Do you hear something I cannot hear? Why do you want to run off? Where do you want to go?' The little lamb just bleated 'Maaa'.

'I have a feeling this night is going to be different from all other nights,' Reuben thought to himself.

The Angels Prepare

The angels were all very excited. But the youngest angels were especially excited.

'Something special must be happening,' said one.

'It must be extra special,' said another, 'because usually only the big angels get to sing in the choir.'

'And this time even us little angels are allowed to sing,' said a third.

'And we're going to learn a special new song too,' said the first angel.

'And you have a lot of practising to do,' said a big angel, 'so come along at once.' The big angel flew off to the choir practice and the little angels followed her.

The big angel was right. They had a lot of preparing to do before the big performance. They had to warm up their voices. 'La, la, la, la,' they sang again and again. They had to find their place in the row they were to sing in. They had to learn their words. They had to learn to start and stop when the big angel gave the sign. They had to be able to open their mouths wide and sing out. And they had to practise and practise and practise.

'I can't wait for whatever it is to happen and then we can sing,' whispered one of the little angels to another.

'I have a feeling it won't be long now,' he whispered back.

'It might even be tonight,' whispered a third.

'Now,' said the big angel in a strict voice. 'Our practising and our preparation are over. This will be a very special night. Line up in your rows and follow me!' And off they went.

The Kings Prepare

Melchior, Caspar and Balthasaar were kings. Sometimes they met together and talked. Sometimes they met together and looked at the stars.

'I don't see any sign of it tonight,' said Melchior.

'No,' said Caspar. 'No bright star in the sky tonight.'

'Not tonight, but soon,' said Balthasaar. 'It will come soon. We must be prepared.'

Next day they met and talked.

'I have saddled my camel. He is ready to go,' said Melchior.

'I have packed my belongings. I am ready to go,' said Caspar.

'I have filled the water bottles and strapped them on to the camel. I am ready to go,' said Balthasaar.

Next night, the three friends met. They did not talk. They sat and looked up into the starry sky. They watched and waited for the bright star to appear. It did not appear.

The next day the three kings met and talked.

'I have packed some gold in my bags, so I am well prepared,' said King Melchior.

'I have packed some frankincense in my bags,' said King Caspar, 'so I am well prepared.'

'I have packed some myrrh in my bags,' said King Balthasaar, 'so I too am well prepared.'

That night the three met. They looked up into the night sky. They looked to the north. No sign of a bright star. They looked to the south. No sign of a bright star. They looked to the west. No sign of a bright star. Finally they looked to the east. 'There it is. The sign we have been waiting for. The bright star,' they shouted.

'Let us go quickly,' said Melchior. 'We must follow the star and not lose sight of it.'

Their camels were ready. Their belongings were ready. Their gifts were ready. They were ready and off they went, following the bright star.

Mary and Joseph Prepare

Everyone in the village of Nazareth was very busy. They were packing bags, they were loading up the donkeys, they were putting parcels of food together, they were closing up their houses and heading off on a long journey to the town where they were born. They were going to write their names in Caesar's book. Mary and Joseph were going to Bethlehem.

Mary and Joseph were preparing to go on the journey too. But they had more packing to do than some of the others. You see, Mary was going to have a baby and so she had to pack some little clothes in case the baby would be born while she and Joseph were in the city. Mary packed some baby clothes and some baby blankets.

Then, together with all the other people from the village of Nazareth, they set off. They travelled a long way. Then they stopped for something to eat.

'How long till we get to Bethlehem, Joseph?' Mary asked.

'Not long now,' said Joseph.

They travelled for another long while. They stopped for a rest. They chatted to their friends.

They travelled for another long time.

'I think the baby will be here soon, Joseph,' said Mary.

'Look! There is Bethlehem,' said Joseph. 'We must write our names in Caesar's book, then we must find a room where we can stay for the night.'

When Mary and Joseph had written their names in the book, they started to look for a room.

'I hope we can find one quickly, Joseph,' said Mary. 'I think the baby will be here soon. We must prepare for the baby, we must unpack the baby clothes and blankets and find a cradle to put the baby in when it arrives.'

Joseph and Mary knocked on the door of every inn in the city. But all the rooms were already full up.

Chatting
Depending on what story(ies) you wish to explore with the children, choose from the following chattings.

Mary and Elizabeth: Mary and Elizabeth were cousins – do you have any cousins? Mary went on a long journey to visit her cousin. Have you ever gone on a long journey to visit someone? Tell us about it. Did you bring any presents? Have you ever helped to choose a present for a new baby? What presents do you think Mary and Elizabeth bought for each other? Do you think Mary enjoyed staying with Elizabeth? Do you think that Elizabeth enjoyed having Mary come to stay?

The shepherds: The shepherds were going to take turns minding the sheep while the others slept. What do you think it was like to work at night in the fields? Do you know anyone who works at night-time? Do you think that the sheep slept during the night? What about the little lambs? Do you like bed-time?

The angels: What were the angels doing? Have you ever sung in a choir or with a group? The little angels were very excited. Why? Were you ever excited?

The three kings: The three kings were going on a long journey. They had to get ready. What kind of things do you think they would have brought with them for the journey? Can you guess where the kings were going?

Chatting about birthdays: Do you know the names of the two babies Mary and Elizabeth were waiting for? Soon we will be celebrating Jesus' birthday. Do you celebrate your birthday? What do you do? On your birthday, those you live with and your friends remember the day you were born. On Christmas Day we will remember and celebrate the day Jesus was born. Now we are preparing for Christmas.

Pupil Book
Chat to the children about the pictures on pages 17 and 18. The picture on page 17 shows Mary and Elizabeth: Which of the women is Elizabeth? Which one is Mary? What do you think Mary's present is? Do you think they are glad to see each other? The picture on page 18 shows us the inside of Rebecca's home – how is it different to the inside of your home? The street is very busy. What can we see?

Video
Watch the final video piece 'All Together' with the children. Chat to them about what they see and hear.

Prayertime
You might like to lead the children in prayer at Advent, using the following Prayertime text.

Sign of the Cross

Leader
We light our candle and we remember that God is always with us.
We ask God to bless us as we prepare to celebrate the birthday of Jesus this Christmas. We pray: God, bless us, we pray.

As we make our Christmas cards.

All
God, bless us, we pray.

Leader
As we send cards to those we love.

All
God, bless us, we pray.

Leader
As we tidy our homes in preparation.

All
God, bless us, we pray.

Leader
As we find the crib.

All
God, bless us, we pray.

Leader
As we find the figures of Mary, Joseph and the baby Jesus for the crib.

All
God, bless us, we pray.

Leader
We pray together:

All
'Thank you, God, for Jesus'
Is the prayer we say.
'Thank you, God, for Jesus'
We pray on Christmas Day.

Sign of the Cross

First Class/Primary Three:
One Moment: Term 1, Lesson 13 (*Alive-O 3*, p. 132)

What am I trying to do?
To help the children to tap into the significant moments in their own experience as they prepare for Christmas.
To introduce them to the story of the Annunciation, an event that marks a significant moment in the biblical infancy narrative.

Why?
So that their preparation for and celebration of Christmas will be more significant.
So that they will come to a deeper understanding of the significance of the birth of Jesus.

Watching, Waiting, Wondering: Term 1, Lesson 14 (*Alive-O 3*, p. 141)

What am I trying to do?
To provide an opportunity for the children to hear again the story of the Three Kings, with an emphasis on waiting, watching and wondering as the birth of Jesus approaches, and to focus the children on their own 'waiting' experiences as Christmas draws near.

Why?
So that they will come to a deeper understanding of the significance of Advent and Christmas.

For your visit choose from the following lesson elements and suggestions:

Song
Sing or invite the children to sing *Mary* or *Following a Star.* Chat to them about the song.

Story
Read or invite the children to tell one or both of the following stories: *One Moment* or *Watching, Waiting, Wondering.*

One Moment
(Adapted from Luke 1:26-38)

One very ordinary day Mary was in the kitchen. The sun was shining in the window and on to the table where she was baking bread. Mary felt happy. As she kneaded the dough, she hummed a little song to herself. Then an unusual thing happened. She had turned around to get some more flour, when suddenly, out of nowhere, an angel stood in the kitchen doorway. Mary jumped.

'Oh!' she remembered saying, almost dropping the flour.

The angel smiled. 'Hello, Mary,' he said. 'My name is Gabriel. Do not be afraid. I have news for you!'

Mary remembered how surprised she was by what the angel had said. 'I hope it's good news,' she said, in a worried voice.

'Don't be afraid, it's wonderful news,' Gabriel replied.

Mary remembered listening to what the angel had to say.

'You are very special, Mary, and God loves you,' Gabriel continued. 'You are going to have a baby – a very special baby boy. His name will be Jesus. He will be God's son.'

Mary was amazed. For a moment she didn't know what to say. So the angel continued...

'And I have more news too, your cousin Elizabeth is also going to have a baby!'

Mary knew Elizabeth had wanted a baby for a long time. She knew Elizabeth would be overjoyed. She knew it would be lovely for her baby to have a little cousin.

She said, 'I know that God cares for me very much. God is very good. I will do whatever God asks.' Then the angel disappeared and Mary went on with her baking, singing her song.

Watching, Waiting, Wondering
(Adapted from Matthew 2:1-3)

Once in the East there lived three kings. They were wise because they watched carefully, they waited endlessly, and they wondered at everything.

They watched the movements of the sun, the moon and the stars, they watched the changes in the weather and the ways of the animals. They looked deep into their own hearts and watched carefully to see what was happening inside themselves.

They waited patiently for those who were slow to move. They waited anxiously when there was nothing else they could do. But most of all, they waited eagerly for the right moment.

As they waited, they wondered. They wondered about the world. They wondered about life. They wondered about themselves.

'There is a new star in the sky tonight,' said Caspar.
'We see that,' said Balthasaar and Melchior.

They watched. They wondered.

'I wonder why there is a new star in the sky?' said Caspar.
'That's what I'm wondering too,' said Balthasaar.
'I wonder if it's a sign?' said Melchior, '...a star-sign.'

They watched. They waited. They wondered.

'Why are we waiting?' asked Balthasaar.
'Because we are wondering,' said Caspar.
'Waiting and wondering go well together,' said Melchior wisely.

They watched. They waited. They wondered.

Just at that moment the star began to move.

'Watch out!' said Melchior. 'The star is moving!'
'I see that,' said Caspar.
'I wonder why it's moving,' said Balthasaar.

They watched. They waited. They wondered.

'If something is moving, you can follow it,' said Caspar, wisely.
'True,' said Melchior. 'You cannot follow something that does not move.'
'Let's watch where this star goes and follow it,' suggested Balthasaar.

They stood up. They saddled their camels. They climbed on board.

'Ready...' said Caspar.
'Steady...' said Melchior.
'Go!' said Balthasaar.

And off they went to follow the star they had watched for, waited for, and
wondered about – to follow wherever it would lead.

Chatting
*Depending on what story(ies) you wish to explore with the children, choose from the
following chattings.*

One Moment: Have you ever heard the story of Mary and the angel Gabriel
before? Tell us about when you heard it. Where was Mary when she began
remembering? When Mary began to think back on the first moment, how do
you think she felt? How did she feel at the end of the story? Have you ever
heard a 'good-news' story? Is this story a 'good-news' story? What good news
did the angel have for Mary? Mary's new baby was to be called Jesus. Do you
know how or why your name was chosen?

Watching, Waiting, Wondering: The three people in the story were called wise.
Do you think they were wise? Do you know anyone who is wise? The people
in the story were waiting for something. What do you think they were

waiting for? The people in the story were wondering about things. What were they wondering? Do you ever wonder about anything? Have you ever wondered why Christmas is such a special time of the year?

Pupil Book
Chat to the children about the pictures on page 18: What is Mary doing? Have you ever made bread? Why is Mary happy? Can you remember what news the angel brought Mary? Pages 20 and 21: Which king do you think is Melchior, Balthasaar, Caspar? What are they doing? What are they getting ready for? Where are they going? Who do you think they will meet at the end of their journey?

Art
The children may be completing artwork in preparation for Christmas. Look at their work and chat to them about it.

Video
Watch the video piece 'Moments' with the children. Chat to them about what they hear and see.

Prayertime
You might like to lead the children in prayer using the following Prayertime text.

Sign of the Cross

Leader *(as the candle, or the appropriate candle on the Advent wreath, is lit)*
God is the light of our life.
The light of all time.

As we ring our bell we know that God is with us now.

Today we remember in prayer the story of the special moment when the angel Gabriel came to Mary. We will stand up and use our bodies along with our voices to pray to God.

Leader *(with children repeating words and actions)*
Hail Mary, full of grace.
(Arms outstretched at the side, palms facing upwards)

The Lord is with thee.
(Arms lifted high above the head)

Blessed art though among women.
(Arms outstretched in front, palms facing upwards)

And blessed is the fruit of thy womb, Jesus.
(Cradle and gently rock the 'baby' in arms)

Sign of the Cross

Second Class/Primary Four:
The People Who Walked in Darkness: Term 1, Lesson 12
(*Alive-O 4*, p. 138)

and

From Darkness to Light: Term 1, Lesson 13 (*Alive-O 4*. p. 154)

What am I trying to do?
To help the children to discover the meaning of Christmas through the account of Jesus' birth as described in Matthew's Gospel.

Why?
So that the season of Advent will be more meaningful for the children and so that they will have a deeper appreciation of Christmas and enter more fully into the Church's celebration of the birth of Jesus.

For your visit choose from the following lesson elements and suggestions:

Song
Sing or invite the children to sing *A Star Shines* or *Following a Star* or *Herod's Song*. Chat to the children about the song.

Story
Read or invite the children to tell one or all of the following stories: *The People Who Walked in Darkness; Dazzledom Part I; Dazzledom Part II.*

The People Who Walked In Darkness
Caspar, Melchior and Balthasaar were three wise men who met together at night to study the stars. One night, as he gazed at the beauty of the night sky, Balthasaar sighed and said, 'It is strange, friends, I have everything I could possibly want in life yet I have a feeling that there must be more to it.'

'More what?' Caspar asked. 'More gold? More food? A bigger place to live in? You already have more – more than you will ever need.'

'What more can there be?' asked Melchior.

Balthasaar thought before answering. 'I don't quite know, but I will find out,' he said determinedly.

Just as he finished speaking a strange thing happened. 'Look! Look!' he shouted excitedly.

'What?' shouted Melchior.

'Where?' shouted Caspar.

'A strange new star-light in the sky. It appeared just as I was speaking,' cried Balthasaar, hopping from one foot to the other in an effort to contain his excitement. 'Bring my camels; make ready a caravan,' Balthasaar shouted to his servants.

'Where are you going?' his two friends asked.

'New stars don't just "happen",' said Balthasaar. 'A special new star in the sky could mean a special new birth, here on earth,' he continued, gathering up his star-gazing instruments. 'Look, this star is moving; it could be leading us to the birthplace of a new leader. I'm going to follow it.' And he rushed off.

'I'm going too,' said Melchior. 'I have spent long enough gazing out at the darkness; now it is time to go out and walk in it, wherever the light leads.'

'I'm coming with you,' Caspar cried. 'I don't really know why – but you are my friends and I trust you. If you go, I go!'

The three men hurried eagerly out into the night. They talked about the star as they travelled; were they the only ones who had seen it? where might it lead them? who might it lead them to? But even with the light of the star to guide them, journeying in the darkness was not easy. They grew tired and weary. One evening as darkness fell and they waited for the star to reappear, Balthasaar said, 'What if the star doesn't come back tonight?'

'Perhaps we have been too hasty in following this star,' Melchior said, 'what if it is a false light leading us on a wild goose chase?'

Silently, Caspar half-wished that it wouldn't come back, then they could give up their difficult journey and return to the comfort and brightness of their homes.

However, just as he was thinking these thoughts, the star reappeared. But tonight, as they followed it, the three wise men came to a city.

'According to my maps, this must be the city of Jerusalem,' said Balthasaar. 'Perhaps we will find a new leader here.'

Dazzledom – Part I
The three wise men spent several days talking to the people in the streets of Jerusalem, asking them where they might find the new leader who was to be born whose star they had been following in the sky. The people of Jerusalem told them that, for a long time now, they had been expecting God to send them a leader, but they did not know where or when this person would be born.

'But we have seen his star rise,' the wise men said.

'Star – what star?' the people asked.

'Every night for weeks now we have followed the light of his star through the darkness. It led us here…'

'All kinds of dangers lurk in the darkness,' the people replied. 'It is not safe to go wandering about in the night. We stay in our homes and close our windows and doors, and if you were wise men, you would do the same.'

'All sorts of truly marvellous things can happen at night too,' said Caspar, 'just look at the moon and the stars for example.'

'And the night brings its own quietness and peace after the busyness of the day,' said Melchior.

'We have come to trust in this new light,' said Balthasaar. 'It has stayed with us, leading us through our dark journey.'

'Talk to Simeon and Anna,' one innkeeper told them. 'They are an old couple who have spent their whole lives praying and watching and waiting for the one whom God will send. You will find them in the temple.'

The wise men went to the temple and talked to Simeon and Anna. 'Has the new leader been here – have you seen him?' they asked.

'Not yet…' said Simeon.

'But it will not be long now,' said Anna.

Soon the whole city was talking about the three odd men who went wandering through the darkness following the light of a new star. The news reached King Herod's palace.

'Who are these three men and what are they doing in my country?' he shouted. 'Send for the chief priests and the scribes and find out what is going on,' he ordered. 'There can be no other leader in Judaea but me.'

The chief priests and scribes, learned men in Jerusalem, told Herod that, according to the prophets of old, a child would be born in the City of David, in Bethlehem. No matter how dark the world, this child's life would bring new light, new hope, and a new kind of leadership to the world. When Herod heard this he became very worried. He sent immediately for the three wise men.

Dazzledom – Part II
'Welcome my friends,' said Herod as the wise men arrived into his huge banqueting hall. 'What brings you to my country?'

'Why! The new light – haven't you seen the light, King Herod?' said Melchior.

'Light!' he shouted. 'What new light? My palace has the brightest light in all of Judaea, light so strong that it banishes darkness.'

And indeed, every evening at the first hint of twilight, a thousand lights were lit throughout the halls of the palace to keep out the night.

'The light of the star,' said Balthasaar.

'Star!' he shouted. 'What star? I am the only real star in Judaea. Look at my palace; look at my feast; look at my star-guests.'

And indeed Herod led a glittering life. He had a magnificent palace with sumptuous food, and was continually surrounded by people just like himself.

'We have talked to the people in the streets,' said Balthasaar, '...they have been waiting for God to send them a leader. We believe this light will lead us to him. This leader will bring new meaning to the lives of people everywhere.'

'There is a leader here already,' said Herod. 'I am he – Herod, King of the Jews. I have an army; I have power and might.' And indeed Herod's power and might was known far and near. 'It must be me you are looking for.'

Balthasaar and Melchior looked at each other. They weren't sure. They spoke quietly among themselves.

'Of course! It must be him!' said Caspar, gazing in wonder at the magnificence of Herod's palace. 'This is exactly the kind of place in which I would expect to find a world leader.'

'I am not so sure,' said Melchior. 'There is light in his palace, it is true, but it is a light that dazzles and blinds. It is not the kind of light one sees by.'

'And he has a magnificent palace with a sumptuous feast before him,' said Balthasaar, 'but only his friends share his fortune and his food.'

Caspar thought for a moment. 'You are right, my friends,' he said, 'King Herod has an army, he has power and might. But the people in the streets are unhappy because he does not lead them. He forces them to go where *he* wants them to go and forces them to do what *he* wants them to do.'

All this time King Herod had been thinking to himself. Maybe they were right. Maybe a new leader had been born. He grew worried and said to the wise men: 'My advice to you is to follow your star, go to Bethlehem and look for your leader there. When you find him, please come back here and tell me about him. I would like to meet this new leader too!'

The three wise men mounted their camels and set off once more. As they passed through the city gates, the star reappeared and moved ahead of them.

Chatting
Depending on what story(ies) you wish to explore with the children, choose from the following chattings.

The People Who Walked in Darkness: In the story why do you think Caspar, Melchior and Balthasaar are called 'wise men'? What makes a person wise? Do you think that the three men were wise to rush off after a star, in the middle of the night? Do you think that the wise men trusted that the star would bring them somewhere or to someone special? Whom do you trust? There is someone else, who is always there to guide us and help us to see our way – can you think who this is?

Dazzledom I and II: In the story *Dazzledom I,* do you think that the wise men were glad to stop at the city? What did the people of the city tell the wise men? What were they waiting for? Have you ever heard the story of Anna and Simeon before? Tell us about the story.

The story continues in *Dazzledom II.* What happens the wise men in this story? Whom do they meet? What kind of leader was Herod? Do you think he was a good leader? What kinds of things should a good leader do for the people?

Chatting about Christmas: Whose birthday are we all waiting to celebrate in a few weeks' time? Why do we celebrate Jesus' birthday each year? Do you celebrate your birthday?

Pupil Book
Chat to the children about the pictures on pages 17, 18 and 19. Read the text with them and chat to them about the wise men.

Activity
You might like to help the children to set up the crib in the classroom. When all the figures are in the crib, you might like to bless the crib for the class.

Video
You might like to watch the video piece 'Christmas'. Chat to the children about what they see and hear.

Prayertime
You might like to lead the children in prayer centred on the Advent season, using the following Prayertime text.

Note: This Prayertime is centred on the Bible as the Word of God. A child is invited to come forward and read a short piece of text from the Bible. Alternatively, you could choose to read the text for the children. Should you choose to invite a child to read the text, the text in question needs to be highlighted clearly to facilitate easy reading. In advance of doing the Bible Procession Ritual, find out from the class teacher if the children are familiar with the format.

Bible Procession Ritual

A child takes the Bible from its place in the classroom and proceeds to a table where the Bible is placed reverently. The child bows and returns to her/his seat.

Leader *(as the candle or the appropriate Advent candle is lit)*
In our winter darkness,
Our Advent candle lights the way.

Sign of the Cross

Leader
As we read from the Bible we remember that the Bible is the Word of God. We know that God is with us in a special way when we read from the Bible. We read how the wise men set out on their journey into the night, following the star, searching for something new.

_____ *(name of child)* will read the Word of God for us today.

The child is invited to come forward. The leader takes the Bible from the table and ceremoniously hands it to the child. The child, holding the Bible, faces the class.

Reader
The Lord be with you.

All
And also with you.

Leader
This reading is from the Gospel according to St Matthew.

All
Glory to you, Lord.

Reader
'In the time of King Herod, after Jesus was born in Bethlehem of Judaea, wise men from the East came to Jerusalem.'

The Gospel of the Lord. *(raising the Bible)*

All
Praise to you, Lord Jesus Christ.

Sign of the Cross

Theme 4: Christmas
Time of Visit: The second last week of December

Scope: All Classes

The celebration of the birth of Jesus at Christmas is central to a religious education programme. Children readily enter into the excitement, the joy and the fuss of the Christmas season. Each year over a series of lessons the children are invited to explore the meaning of Christmas at a deeper level than that of the commercial, which draws them and many adults into its attractions. The opportunity to engage the children in a chatting about the true meaning of the season of Christmas should not be passed over.

Junior Infants/Primary One:
Jesus is Born: Term 1, Lesson 15 (*Alive-O*, p. 109)

What am I trying to do?
To introduce the children to the story of the birth of Jesus.

Why?
So that they will link their experience of celebrating Christmas with the birth of Jesus.

For your visit choose from the following lesson elements and suggestions:

Song
Sing or invite the children to sing *Mary*. You might like to sing some other Christmas carols with/for the children.

Story
Read or invite the children to tell the story *The Waiting is Over*. Invite the children to retell stories they have heard during Advent: *Anna; Simeon; Anna and Simeon; Mary and Joseph go on a Journey*.

The Waiting is Over
When Mary and Joseph and the donkey reached the cave, they went inside. Now all their waiting was almost over. They were not very long there when the time came for the baby to be born. Mary gave birth to a baby. It was a little baby boy. Mary and Joseph were very, very happy.

'He is beautiful,' said Joseph, taking the baby in his arms.

Mary kissed the new baby and said, 'His name is Jesus.'

Then Joseph wrapped the baby in a little blanket and looked around for somewhere to lay him.

'Look Joseph,' said Mary, 'there's a manger. The animals eat their food out of it. It looks almost like a cradle. Perhaps we can lay the baby there.'

Joseph put some hay in the bottom of the manger, to make it nice and soft for the baby. Then he put Jesus in it.

Meanwhile the shepherds were hurrying to see the wonderful thing that the angels had told them about. As they walked along they chatted excitedly.

'What do you think we will find?' asked one.

'I don't know,' said a second, 'but the angels said it was something wonderful.'

'But we must find the cave first,' said a third. 'I can hardly wait.'

'Me too,' said all the other shepherds together.

When they arrived at the cave, they could hardly believe their eyes. There, lying in a manger, was a beautiful new baby.

'It is exactly as the angels told us,' they said. 'This is a very special baby.'

'His name is Jesus,' said Joseph.

There were three magi who lived in a country far, far away from Bethlehem. They were waiting for the news that Jesus was born. When a very bright star appeared in the sky, they knew that it must be the time. They fed their camels and gave them water for a long journey. They chose presents to give to Jesus.

Then they slowly made their way to Bethlehem on their camels. They were following a star. They came to the cave and went in. They saw Mary, Joseph and the baby.

Chatting
Chatting about the story 'The Waiting is Over': Why were Mary and Joseph very happy? Were you ever very happy? What makes you happy? What did Mary call the baby? Where did the baby sleep? Who came to visit the baby? What did the shepherds say to one another as they walked along? What sort of men came on camels? What sort of an animal is a camel? Would you like to take a ride on a camel? Why are babies special? Why is Jesus special?

Pupil Book
Chat to the children about the picture on page 18: Look at the baby. Do you like this baby? Who is looking at the baby? What do you think they are saying? What do you think the baby Jesus is looking at? Who are the people behind Jesus? If you could see their faces, do you think they would be looking happy or sad? What would you like to say to the baby Jesus?

Video

If you have not already shown the piece of the video which is built around the song *The Carol of the Journey,* now might be a good time to watch it with the children. This can be found in the section 'We Belong'.

Art

Ask to see the artwork that the children may have done in the weeks coming up to Christmas.

Christmas Play

You might like to view the children doing their Christmas play.

Prayertime

You might like to lead the children in a prayer around the crib, using the following Prayertime text.

Note: *Gather the children around the crib so that they can all see the figures.*

Sign of the Cross

Light the candle.

Leader
As we look at the crib we remember all those who were there on the first Christmas night when Jesus was born. We think of Mary, the mother of Jesus. She looked after Jesus when he was a baby. She fed him and loved him and cared for him. She taught him his first words. She helped him to take his first steps. She told him stories and taught him to say his prayers.

We thank God for Mary.

All
Thank you, God, for Mary.

Leader
We see Joseph. With Mary he looked after Jesus when he was a baby. Joseph loved Jesus. He taught him to do many things. He would have taught him how to eat with a spoon, how to write, how to count. When he got bigger, Joseph would have taught Jesus the names of the flowers and the trees and the plants in the countryside around where they lived.

We thank God for Joseph.

All
Thank you, God, for Joseph.

Leader
We see Jesus. Jesus was born on the first Christmas night. He came to earth to show us how much God loves us and cares for us. When he was a tiny baby,

he needed to be cared for as every baby needs to be cared for. He wasn't able to feed himself or dress himself. He couldn't walk or talk. Mary and Joseph took care of him. Jesus came to tell us that God always loves us and cares for us.

We thank God for Jesus.

All
'Thank you, God, for Jesus',
Is the prayer we say.
'Thank you, God, for Jesus'
We pray on Christmas Day.

Sign of the Cross

Senior Infants/Primary Two:
Celebrating the Birth of Jesus: Term 1, Lesson 15
(*Alive-O 2*, p. 125)

What am I trying to do?

To deepen the children's knowledge of and love for the story of the birth of Jesus.

Why?

So that they will link their experience of preparing for the celebration of Christmas with the birth of Jesus.

For your visit choose from the following lesson elements and suggestions:

Song

Sing or invite the children to sing *Away in a Manger* or *Mary*. You might like to sing other Christmas carols with them.

Story

Read or invite the children to tell the story *Jesus is Born*.

Jesus is Born

Mary and Joseph tried one last time to get a room. They knocked at Rebecca's door.

'If that is someone else looking for a room, tell them we are full up,' said Rebecca's mother, when she heard the knock.

Rebecca opened the door.

'Please,' said Joseph, 'do you have a room where we can stay for the night? I am Joseph from Nazareth and this is Mary. Mary's baby will be born very soon. We need to find a room.'

Rebecca looked at Mary and Joseph. 'I'm afraid our rooms are all full up,' she replied. 'You will have to try somewhere else.'

'We have tried everywhere,' said Mary.

'I'm sorry,' Rebecca said again. She was just about to shut the door when she remembered the feeling she had that something special was going to happen. 'This woman is going to have a baby,' she thought to herself. 'That is something special.'

'I will help you,' she said. 'We have a cave just outside the city. The animals shelter there when it is cold. You are welcome to stay there.' She told them how to get to the cave.

'Thank you, Rebecca,' said Mary and Joseph, and off they went.

'Alright angels, this is it,' called out the big angel. 'We have arrived.'

'I don't see anything,' said one little angel to another, 'only a hillside with some sheep and some shepherds.'

'Take your places and get ready to sing at the top of your voices,' said the big angel. 'This is a very special occasion. Tonight is a very special night. Tonight a very special baby will be born. I want you to sing and celebrate his birth.'

'I don't care if it's only a hillside,' said another little angel. 'I'm so happy that this special baby will be born. I am happy just to sing and sing and sing.'

'One, two, three,' counted the big angel and all together they sang. *(They sing two verses of the* Alive-O *song, substituting the words Good News for Alive-O.)*

Reuben was fast asleep beside his little lamb. Suddenly he heard singing. At first he thought he was dreaming. He sat up and rubbed the sleep from his eyes. Reuben couldn't make out where the noise was coming from. He looked all around him. He couldn't see anything. Then he looked up to the sky.

'I've never seen anything like it. I've never heard anything like it either,' he said. His little lamb was watching and listening too. Suddenly he ran off.

'Hey, hey, come back here little lamb,' shouted Reuben. He was just going to run after him and bring him back when he realised that all the shepherds were running after the lamb too. 'What's happening,' thought Reuben. Then he remembered the feeling he had had, that this night would be different from all other nights. 'A choir of angels singing in the sky – that makes this night different,' he said. And he ran after the others.

The three kings followed the bright star up hill and down hill, night after night. They weren't quite sure where the star was leading them, but they knew that if they followed it they would see something very special. Soon the bright star moved towards the city of Bethlehem.

'Perhaps the wonderful thing we are to see is in the city,' said King Melchior.

'Perhaps the wonderful thing we are to see is a powerful king who lives in a big palace in the city,' said King Caspar.

'No,' said King Balthasaar. 'It will not be a powerful king in a fine palace, because look….' He pointed to the sky. 'The bright star is moving again. We must hurry after it.' And they did.

Then the star stopped. It shone its bright light on a cave on the hillside. The kings hurried inside the cave. There they saw Mary, Joseph and a newborn baby boy. The baby was wrapped in a blanket and he was lying in a manger. There were shepherds in the cave and Reuben was there with his little lamb. A choir of angels sang a song. King Melchior gave the baby the gold he had brought. King Caspar gave him a present of the frankincense and King Balthasaar gave him the myrrh. Everyone agreed that this was a very special night. It was the night Baby Jesus was born.

Chatting

Chatting about the story: What happened when Mary and Joseph arrived in Bethlehem? What were they looking for? Did they find a place to sleep? Why did the angels sing? What sort of songs do you sing? What sort of songs do we sing at Christmas time? Will we sing a Christmas song now? What did the shepherd and the three kings find when they arrived at the cave? Do you think they were excited and surprised? How do you think Mary would have welcomed them? This night was very special – why?

Pupil Book

Chat to the children about the picture on pages 20 and 21: What do you think of Mary's new baby? Can you name all the people in the picture? Do you know what presents the kings brought? If you were to bring a present to the baby Jesus that night, what would you have brought?

Art

If the children have completed artwork celebrating the theme of Christmas you might like to look at it and chat to them about their work.

Video

If you have not already done so, watch the section of the video that focuses on Christmas with the children. Chat to them about what they see and hear. The piece can be found at the end of the section 'All Together'.

Prayertime

You might like to lead the children in prayer around the crib, using the following Prayertime text.

Sign of the Cross

Leader

We light our candle and we remember that God is always with us.
God is with us as we celebrate the birthday of Jesus.

Close your eyes.
Place your hands gently on your lap.
Place your feet on the floor.
Listen to your heart beat.
Feel your breath as it goes gently in and out of your lungs.

Go into your little inside world where it's dark and safe and quiet and peaceful. In there you can feel safe and secure. There is no one in there in your little inside space except yourself and anyone you wish to invite in. If you wish, you can invite Jesus into your little world this Christmas. You can talk to Jesus. You can say anything you wish to Jesus. With your little inside voice, which no one else except Jesus can hear, you can tell Jesus that you love him. You can ask Jesus to take care of you. You can say happy birthday to Jesus. You can ask Jesus to look after all the people whom you love this Christmas.

When you are finished speaking to Jesus you can open your eyes again. Together we sing:

All *(sing)*
Away in a Manger/Mary

Sign of the Cross

First Class/Primary Three:
The Moment They'd all Been Waiting For: Term 1, Lesson 15
(*Alive-O 3*, p. 151)

What am I trying to do?
To deepen the children's appreciation of and love for the Christmas event.

Why?
So that the children will come to a deeper understanding of the birth of Jesus as the focus of all the moments, preparations and waiting that make up the Advent season.

For your visit choose from the following lesson elements and suggestions:

Song
Sing or invite the children to sing *This is the Moment* or *Away in a Manger* or *Carol of the Journey.* Chat to the children about the song.

Story
Read or invite the children to tell the story *The Moment They'd all Been Waiting For.*

The Moment They'd All Been Waiting For
(Adapted from Luke 2:1-20)

A man called Caesar Augustus was a Roman emperor. He was 'in charge'. One day, he decided to count and see how many people he was in charge of. He sent soldiers throughout the land to give people this message. Every family must go to the town their ancestors had come from. There they must write the names of all those in their family into a special book. All the books in all the towns throughout the land were then to be collected and Caesar would count all the names. In this way he would find out how many people he was in charge of.

When Joseph heard the instructions he told Mary that the two of them would have to go from Nazareth to the town of his ancestor, King David. *(Do you remember the story of David from last year? The shepherd boy who became king of his people.)* Joseph's ancestors had lived in Bethlehem. As they travelled along the way to Bethlehem, Mary wondered whether Joseph would have two names or three names to write in Caesar's book. You see, Mary was going to have a baby. She wasn't sure of the exact moment her baby would be born, but she knew it would be soon.

When Mary and Joseph reached the city there was a long queue of people waiting to sign their names in Caesar's book.

As they stood in the queue, Mary and Joseph heard people talking and whispering. 'Some day we will have a true leader,' said a cross young woman, 'one of our own who will show everyone how to treat people fairly and justly.'

A young man beside her shook his head. 'We have been promised such a leader for a long time now,' he said bitterly, 'but there is no sign of him yet. How much longer do we have to wait?'

'Stop talking! Move along!' shouted the soldiers roughly.

'Well, whenever he comes, it will not be a moment too soon,' said the cross young woman.

Joseph and Mary signed their names in the book and went off to look for somewhere to stay. But with all the crowds in town, the only place they could find to stay in was a cave out on the hillside. It was getting closer and closer to the moment when Mary's baby would be born.

Out on the hills around Bethlehem some shepherds were rushing to gather their flocks together for the night. As they set about gathering their flocks they talked about the time when a new leader would come among them.

'But how will we know when this person that we have waited so long for has finally come?' asked Reuben, the youngest shepherd.

'There will be a sign,' said Isaac, the oldest shepherd. 'We do not know what kind of sign it will be, but when it comes, we will recognise it.'

At that very moment on a hillside outside Bethlehem, Mary's baby boy cried for the first time. The moment Mary and Joseph had been waiting for was finally here. The baby was born.

At that very same moment, the sign the shepherds had talked about was given; the sky above them was filled with the sound of angels singing. 'Go and see the new baby,' the angels told the shepherds.

And at that same moment the three wise ones mounted their camels and set off to follow a new star that had appeared in the sky. It brought them to a hillside where they found a cave. Inside the cave, shepherds were bowed down before a baby who lay in a manger. The baby's mother smiled at the three wise ones.

'You are just in time,' she said, showing them the new baby. 'This is the moment we have all been waiting for!'

Chatting
Chatting about the story: All the people in the story were waiting for someone special to come. They didn't know about Mary's baby. What sort of person do you think they had in mind when they talked of 'someone special' who had

been promised? Do you think that Mary knew that her baby was very special? Who came to visit the baby Jesus? Why do you think the shepherds and the wise men came?

Pupil Book
Chat to the children about the picture on pages 22 and 23: What is everybody doing in the picture? What is happening in your home at this time of year? Who are the figures in the crib? What are they doing? Do you have a crib in your home? How might you go about putting up a crib in your home?

Art
If the children have completed artwork celebrating the season of Christmas, you might like to look at it and chat to them about it.

Christmas Play
You might like to invite the children to do some of the Christmas play for you.

Video
If you have not already shown the video piece 'Moments', which deals with Advent and Christmas, you might like to do so now. Chat to the children about what they see and hear.

Prayertime
You might like to lead the children in a prayer around the crib, using the following Prayertime text.

Note: If possible and in consultation with the class teacher, place the empty crib in a prominent position.

Sign of the Cross

Leader (as the candle, or appropriate candles on the Advent wreath, is lit)
Glory to God in the highest
And peace to his people on earth.

The crib reminds us of the first Christmas. Today we are going to ask God to bless our classroom crib as we remember the Christmas story.

Bless our crib, O God.
Our crib tells us the Christmas story about...

When Mary and Joseph could not find a place to stay in town.

All
Bless our crib, O God.

Leader
How they found room in a cave.

The figures are placed in the crib by two children who then bow reverently and return to their seats.

All
Bless our crib, O God.

Leader
How the animals kept them warm and safe.

Children come forward and place the animals in the crib, bow reverently and return to their seats.

All
Bless our crib, O God.

All *(sing)*
Away in a Manger

Sign of the Cross

Second Class/Primary Four:
Jesus – A Light for All: Term 1, Lesson 14 (*Alive-O 4*, p. 166)

What am I trying to do?
To help the children to discover the meaning of Christmas through the account of Jesus' birth as described in Matthew's Gospel.

Why?
So that the season of Advent will be more meaningful for the children and so that they will have a deeper appreciation of Christmas and enter more fully into the Church's celebration of the birth of Jesus.

For your visit choose from the following lesson elements and suggestions:

Song
Sing or invite the children to sing *Mary's Lullaby* or *Silent Night*. You might like to sing other Christmas carols with the children.

Story
Read or ask the children to tell *The Christmas Story*.

The Christmas Story
As the three wise men left the city, the star reappeared. They followed it into a rocky hill-region full of caves.

'Caves!' said Caspar, in surprise. 'Surely no one would be born in a cave!'

'Don't forget, Caspar,' said Balthasaar, 'we have been in the splendour of Herod's palace and we did not find what we were looking for there.'

But Melchior was not listening to his two friends. He had become very excited. 'Look! Look!' he exclaimed. 'The star has stopped over there. It is shining on that little cave-dwelling in the side of the hill.'

The wise men rode towards the cave and clambered down from their camels. Melchior and Balthasaar approached the entrance. Caspar hesitated.

'It looks very dark in there,' he whispered anxiously.

As if in an effort to reassure him, the star shone its light in the entrance of the cave.

'Thank you, Star,' said Caspar, tip-toeing closer.

The three wise men listened. Someone was singing a Jewish song. It sounded like a lullaby.

'Sounds like someone is putting a baby to sleep, we had better go softly,' Balthasaar whispered.

Softly and quietly the three tip-toed into the cave. The echoes and the shadows almost made it seem as though the cave itself was singing.

But of course it was not. A young woman was singing to her baby. The wise men gazed in wonder and awe and silence at what they saw. As she finished singing, a man stepped out of the shadows. 'Shalom,' he said, 'I am Joseph. This is Mary and this is the new baby. You are welcome to share this cave and anything we have – our food, our fire, our company, and especially our joy.'

The wise men introduced themselves and told the story of how they had followed the star all the way to this very cave.

Then Joseph told the story of how an angel had told him that Mary would have a very special child and that his name would be Immanuel.

'It means "God is with us",' Mary said.

'Where or when or how? Where or when or how is God with us?' Caspar asked, puzzled.

Mary said, 'Right here and now, in the birth of my son, God is with us. In light and darkness, in sorrow and joy, in peace and trouble, in every moment everywhere, God is with us.'

Balthasaar took the baby in his arms. 'Now I have found what I have been looking for,' he said, smiling peacefully. 'Never again will I want or need anything more.'

Then the wise men gave the baby gifts they had brought for the new leader – gold, frankincense and myrrh.

Chatting
Chatting about the story: Have you ever heard this story before? Why do we tell this story each year? Do you think the story is a good way to remember Jesus' birthday? Do you have any stories you tell again and again? We remember Jesus' birthday by telling the Christmas story. How else can we remember Jesus' birthday? Mary and Joseph shared the warmth of the cave with their visitors – what do you and I share at Christmas? Do you think that Mary and Joseph shared their joy and excitement with the visitors? How can we share in Mary's joy at Christmas time?

Pupil Book
Chat to the children about the picture and text on pages 20 and 21.

Art
You might like to ask the children to show you some artwork that they have done in the weeks coming up to Christmas.

Video
Watch the video piece 'Christmas' if you have not already done so. Chat to the children about what they see and hear.

Prayertime
You might like to lead the children in a short Bible Procession Ritual, using the following Prayertime text.

Note: This Prayertime is centred on the Bible as the Word of God. A child is invited to come forward and read a short piece of text from the Bible. Alternatively, you could choose to read the text for the children. Should you choose to invite a child to read the text, the text in question needs to be highlighted clearly to facilitate easy reading. In advance of doing the Bible Procession Ritual, find out from the class teacher if the children are familiar with the format.

Bible Procession Ritual
A child takes the Bible from its place in the classroom and proceeds to a table where the Bible is placed reverently. The child bows and returns to her/his seat.

Leader *(as the candle or the appropriate Advent candle is lit)*
In our winter darkness
Our Advent candle lights the way.

Sign of the Cross

Leader
As we read from the Bible we remember that the Bible is the Word of God. We know that God is with us in a special way when we read from the Bible. We read how the wise men followed the star until it stopped over a cave. In that cave they found the baby Jesus, with Mary and Joseph.

_____ *(name of child)* will read the Word of God for us today.

The child is invited to come forward. The leader takes the Bible from the table and ceremoniously hands it to the child. The child, holding the Bible, faces the class.

Reader
The Lord be with you.

All
And also with you.

Reader
This reading is from the Gospel according to St Matthew.

All
Glory to you, Lord.

Reader
'When they saw that the star had stopped they were full of joy. On entering

the house they saw the child with Mary, his mother; and they knelt down before him.'

The Gospel of the Lord. *(raising the Bible)*

All
Praise to you, Lord Jesus Christ.

Note: If time allows, you might like to invite other children to come forward, raise the Bible and read from the scriptures.

Sign of the Cross

Theme 5: Special Places; Lent
Time of Visit: Six weeks before Easter

Theme 5 offers a different focus for Junior and Senior Infants/Primary One and Two (Special Places) and for First and Second Class/Primary Three and Four (Lent).

Special Places
Scope: Junior Infants/Primary One and
Senior Infants/Primary Two

Lessons such as 'Families Celebrate' and 'A Place to Celebrate' in *Alive-O* and 'Peace Around Me', 'Peace Within Me' and 'Special Places' in *Alive-O 2* lay the foundation for an understanding of Christian celebration and ritual. They introduce the children to the local church building as a special place, a place of prayer, a place of celebration and worship. These lessons offer a wide variety of possibilities for meaningful engagement with children around their knowledge of the church building and their understanding of Christian worship.

Lent
Scope: First Class/Primary Three and
Second Class/Primary Four

Lent is a classic time for reflection and examination – as individuals and as members of the Christian community. Each year at this point of the liturgical calendar Christians are encouraged to stand back a little and to take a closer look at life and all its rhythms. It is a time when the Church nudges us towards a more heightened awareness of our relationship with one another, with our world and with God. *Alive-O 3* and *Alive-O 4* deal specifically with the season of Lent.

Special Places

Junior Infants/Primary One:
Families Celebrate: Term 2, Lesson 6 (*Alive-O*, p. 156)

What am I trying to do?
To help the children become more aware of the times and reasons for celebration which are part of the life of a family.

Why?
So that they will begin to recognise the meaning and significance of moments of celebration in the family, a foundation for a future understanding of the sacraments.

The Church: A Place to Celebrate: Term 2, Lesson 7 (*Alive-O*, p. 163)

What am I trying to do?
To introduce the children to the local church building.

Why?
So that they will be aware of the church as a special place, a place of prayer, a place of celebration.

For your visit choose from the following lesson elements and suggestions:

Song
Sing or invite the children to sing *The Friendly Game* or *Church*.

Story
Read or invite the children to tell one or both of the following stories: *Annie Loves Surprises* or *Celebrating in Church*.

Annie Loves Surprises
Tomorrow would be Annie's birthday. If there was one thing Annie loved about birthdays, it was a surprise. If there was another thing Annie loved about birthdays, it was guessing the surprise. So, even though it wasn't her birthday yet...

Annie searched in the hall.
Annie searched upstairs.
She searched under beds,
took the cushions off the chairs.
But not a sign could Annie find,
neither here nor there,
of a present for her birthday
any, anywhere.

'I hope my family haven't forgotten all about my birthday,' Annie said to herself. 'That would make me very, very sad. And,' she said, thinking things over, 'I'm not sure if I like surprises any more.' Then Annie remembered the wonderful birthday her brother Andy had, with a big birthday cake and candles to blow out. She remembered the fun she had, helping her big sister to make the cake and put icing on it. So, she set off searching again...

Annie searched the cupboards.
Annie searched all the tins.
Opened all the biscuit boxes,
searched inside the breadbin.
But not a sign could Annie find,
neither here nor there,

of a birthday cake with candles
any, anywhere.

'I think my family have forgotten my birthday,' she said sadly to herself. 'I think they don't love me any more. And,' she said in a cross voice, 'I don't like surprises.' Then she remembered the party she had helped her brother Andy to prepare when it was Mam's birthday. She remembered decorating the table, and putting flowers on it. Granny and Grandad said the table looked beautiful. Annie was very proud. So, she set off searching again…

Annie searched the house.
Annie searched the shed.
She searched in all the cubby-holes,
she searched in under the beds.
But not a sign could Annie find,
neither here nor there,
of things for a birthday party
any, anywhere.

Annie was very disappointed. 'I'm very, very sad,' she told herself. 'I'm the only one in the whole house that's remembered my birthday. Poor me. I shall have to celebrate my birthday all by myself. I HATE surprises!'

That night when Annie went to sleep she dreamt that it was her birthday – but it wasn't a very happy birthday. There was no one else at the party except Annie. She blew out the candles all by herself, in one go, but there was no one to clap and cheer. She sang 'Happy Birthday to You' all by herself, because there was no one to join in. She played musical chairs but it was no fun because Annie had lots of empty chairs to sit on. There was no one to help her eat the cake and crisps and treats and to help her drink up all the lemonade, so she had to do it all by herself and very soon her tummy became terribly sick.

'Oooh, oooh, oooh, sore tummy, sore tummy,' Annie cried out in her sleep.

'Annie, Annie, wake up, it's your birthday today,' said Mam, shaking Annie gently. 'Surprise, surprise – see what we have for you.' Annie blinked her eyes and yawned sleepily.

'Happy Birthday to you.
Happy Birthday to you.
Happy Birthday, dear Annie.
We all love you!' sang her family all together.

Annie jumped out of bed and tore the wrapping paper off her present. 'I'm so happy,' she cried, 'you didn't forget… oh, it's beautiful… it's the nicest one I've ever seen… thank you all very much! I LOVE surprises!'

Celebrating in Church

Simon's mammy had got a new baby. Simon had got a new baby too. Auntie Liz had given him a new teddy bear. His daddy and mammy hadn't decided what to call the new baby. Simon couldn't make up his mind what to call his new baby bear. He thought about Teddy or Charlie or Jimmy Joe, but he couldn't make up his mind. Simon's mammy had to feed her new baby. Simon had to feed his baby too. His daddy had to put the new baby to bed. Simon put his new baby to bed and then climbed in beside him.

'Goodnight, baby,' whispered Simon. 'Tomorrow will be a big day.'

Soon baby bear and Simon and Mammy and Daddy and the new baby were fast asleep.

Next morning, the new baby began to cry. Daddy got up to make a bottle. Mammy got up to change the baby's nappy. Simon woke up. He took his baby in his arms and rocked him to and fro. Then he rubbed his back gently in case his baby had wind.

'Big day, today, baby bear,' he said, 'we're going to church to get you a new name of your very own. How would you like Billy, or Harry, or maybe Benny or...'.

'Good clothes today, Simon,' said Mammy. 'It's a special occasion'.

'But my baby hasn't got any good clothes,' said Simon.

'Never mind,' Daddy told Simon. 'Maybe your baby doesn't want to go to church. He can stay at home.'

But Simon did mind. And his baby did want to go to church. The doorbell rang and in came Granny and Grandad, Auntie Flo, Auntie Liz, Uncle Joe and Mrs Frazier from next door. They were all dressed up in their good clothes and Granny had a hat on. She was carrying a big box with a special cake inside.

'Ready, Simon?' asked Grandad. Simon said nothing. He was thinking.

Then the back door opened and in came Cousin Anne, Cousin Sam and Mr Reynolds from across the street. They were all dressed up. Mr Reynolds had a long round box with a candle inside.

'Ready, Simon?' asked Cousin Sam. Simon said nothing. He was thinking. He went to his room and closed the door.

Mammy wrapped a white shawl around the new baby and Daddy carried him out to the car.

'Ready, Simon?' shouted Mammy.

'In a minute,' Simon shouted back.

101

'Then you had better go with Granny and Grandad,' Daddy called out as he drove off to the church.

'Ready, Simon?' asked Granny.

'Ready, now, Granny,' answered Simon, following Granny out to the car, and carrying a bag behind his back.

When they arrived at the church, everyone was waiting. The priest came to the door and said, 'This is a very special day. You are all very welcome to God's house, for this special celebration. Come inside.'

'What's in the bag, Simon?' whispered Auntie Liz.

'Oh, nothing, really,' said Simon.

'What name have you chosen for the new baby?' the priest asked.

As quick as a flash, Simon reached into the bag and took out his baby, all dressed up in a clean white babygro, a little hat on his head and wrapped in a little blanket from the other baby's cot.

'I want to call him Teddy,' said Simon, 'Teddy Bear. That's his name.'

Chatting

Chatting about celebrating at home: When do you have a celebration at home? What do you do at a celebration? Do you eat special food? Do you sing special songs? What sort of special things might you do?

Chatting about the story 'Annie Loves a Surprise': What present do you think Annie got for her birthday? Did you ever get a surprise? Tell us about it. Do you like giving surprises? What's the best thing about having a birthday? Who helps you celebrate your birthday? What is the best thing about having a family and people who love you?

Chatting about the story 'Celebrating in Church': Did anyone ever take you to church to celebrate a new baby? Who was there? What did you do? What name did the baby get? Do you remember anything that happened in the church? Did you ever go to church to celebrate two people getting married? Did you ever go to church to celebrate when one of your sisters or brothers were celebrating their First Communion or their Confirmation? Do you remember anything about the celebration?

Chatting about the local church: Is your church old or new? What do you think it's made of? What shape is it? Is the church bigger or smaller than your home? Why is the church so big? What do you like about it? Do you know the name of your local church? Have you ever seen the windows in the church? What are the windows in the classroom like? Are the windows in the church the same or different from the school windows? Have you ever seen the inside of a church? Can you name any of the things inside the church? What do you call the place where the holy water is kept? What do we do with holy water? What is the big table in the church called? Where do people sit in church? Are there any lights in the church? Do you know the name for the special red light in church? Do you know the name of the place where the Communion is kept?

Pupil Book
Chat to the children about the picture on page 30: Where is the little girl? What colours are in the window? What are all the different things you can see in the window? Have you ever seen a window like that?

Art
You might like to ask the children to show you some of the artwork that they have done recently in Religion class.

Video
Watch the piece of video where the children are enjoying themselves at a birthday party. This can be found at the end of the piece 'I am Special'.

Visit to the local church
In consultation with the class teacher you might like to arrange to take the children on a tour of the local church, showing them the furniture that has been explored in class. In this case you could pray with the children in church, using the format outlined below.

In class the children learn a short prayer to say in church. They also learn to genuflect. You might like to chat to them about this gesture and prayer.

Prayertime *(in the church or in the classroom)*
Sign of the Cross

Light candle as usual.

Leader
Today we give thanks to God our Father for all the happy times of celebration we have with our families and for the people we celebrate with.

For happy times at home.

All
Thank you, God, we pray.

Leader
For birthday parties.

All
Thank you, God, we pray.

Leader
For weddings.

All
Thank you, God, we pray.

Leader
For new babies.

All
Thank you, God, we pray.

Leader
For First Holy Communion.

All
Thank you, God, we pray.

Leader
For Baptism.

All
Thank you, God, we pray.

Leader
For the sad things at home when we know that you are with us.

All
Thank you, God, we pray.

Leader
We know that God is with us in the bad times and the good times.

All
Glory be to the Father,
And to the Son,
And to the Holy Spirit;
As it was in the beginning,
Is now and ever shall be,
World without end. Amen.

Sign of the Cross

Senior Infants/Primary Two:
Special Places: Term 2, Lesson 6 (*Alive-O 2,* p. 175)

What am I trying to do?
To help the children come to a sense of some places as special places, and more particularly of the church as a special place.

Why?
So that they will recognise that in human life there are places of significance and that among these places is the place of worship.
So that they will have an attitude of reverence for the church building and begin to feel at home in it.

For your visit choose from the following lesson elements and suggestions:

Song
Sing or invite the children to sing *The Church.* Chat to them about the song.

Story
Read or invite the children to tell the story *Three Guesses.*

Three Guesses
Maggie and Michael are playing a game. It is a guessing game. Michael is trying to guess Maggie's favourite place in the whole world.

'Give me a clue,' he says. 'Is it outside the trailer or inside?'

'Both,' says Maggie.

Michael is puzzled. He thinks hard. He thinks about outside places that Maggie likes. 'She likes birds and trees and nests,' he says to himself. 'Sometimes when we travel around the country, she finds a nest in a tree. Then she is very happy. But, Maggie says her special place is outside and inside. How could a nest be inside?' Michael looks at Maggie. She is sitting on her bunk – the top bunk. She has gathered the cover around her and has made a little nest out of it. She is cheep, cheep, cheeping. 'Look at me, I'm a sparrow,' she cries, clapping her arms. Michael usually slept in the bottom bunk, but he liked the top one better.

'I know it, I know it,' shouts Michael excitedly.

'Your special place is a nest.'

'Wrong,' laughs Maggie. 'One guess gone.'

Michael thinks hard. He looks all around, inside and out. He sees the biscuit box on the shelf. 'Maggie loves biscuits – she even hides them sometimes,' thinks Michael. 'There is a biscuit box inside – but I don't think there's one outside – unless…' Michael smiles. Maggie had little secret hiding places all around the halting site. 'Maybe she has a biscuit box hidden outside too,' he says to himself.

'I know now,' he says. 'Your special place is the biscuit box.'

'Wrong,' laughs Maggie. 'One guess left.'

'What will I get if I win this game?' asks Michael.

Maggie knew he had only one guess left. She was sure he would not win. 'You can have anything you want that belongs to me,' she promises.

Michael thinks hard. He looks all around. Just then Dad came home in the van. Maggie jumps down and runs to meet him. She jumps into his arms. He lifts her up on his shoulders.

'Look at me. I'm on top of the world,' she cheers. Dad picks Michael up too. Suddenly Michael guesses where Maggie's special place is.

'I know where it is – it's… *(ask the children if they've guessed)* it's up on Daddy's shoulders!' shouts Michael.

'Right,' says Maggie. 'How did you know?'

'Now you have to give me whatever I want,' says Michael.

'What do you want then?' Maggie asks.

'I want to have my special place,' Michael tells her. 'I want to sleep in the top bunk tonight.' And he did.

Chatting

Chatting about the story: Do you have a special place? Tell us about it. Do you have a special place in school? Let's think of special places that are small. Let's think of special places that are big. Do you think our school is a special place? Do you think that the church is a special place? What do you think is special about our local church? Do you have a special place in the church?

Chatting about special items in the church: Do you have **candles** at home? Can you think of times when we use candles? Have you ever seen candles in the church? Tell us about the candles you have seen. Do you know the names of any special church candles? There is a special **red light** in the church – have you ever noticed it? Were you ever in church when your baby brother or sister was being christened/baptised? Tell us about the day? Do you know the name of the special place that holds the **holy water** that is used in Baptism? Every church has a crucifix. Do you know what a **crucifix** is? Have you ever seen one? When we look at a crucifix we remember Jesus. What sort of sound does a **bell** make? Let's think of all the different bells that we know. Do you have a school bell? Have you ever heard the church bell ring? Do you have a table in your home? What is it used for? How many people can sit around your table at home? What happens when we sit down together? The church has a table too – it has a special name. Do you know what its name is? Sometimes we make our table at home special by putting a special cloth on it – what is the cloth called? The **altar** in church has a special cloth too – do you know what it is called?

Pupil Book
Chat to the children about the picture on page 31: What can you see in the picture? Chat to the children about the colour and shape of the various church items.

Video
Watch the section of the video where the priest shows the children around the church. This can be found at the end of section 'Quiet and Still'. Chat to the children about the things they see. If it is not possible to bring the children on a visit to the local church, the video is an excellent way of helping children to become familiar with the inside of a church.

Visit to a church
In consultation with the class teacher you might like to arrange to invite the children to the local church and show them the various items in the church. You could gather the children around the altar at the end of the visit and pray with them using the following Prayertime.

Prayertime
You might like to pray with the children and give thanks to God for our church, using the following Prayertime text.

Sign of the Cross

Leader
Today we are going to thank God for our church.
Our church is a special place.
It's a place where we go to pray. We can go there at any time. Everyone can go there – young people, children, mams and dads, grans and grandads.

We give thanks to God for our church, a special place of prayer.

All
Thank you, God, we pray.

Leader
We give thanks to God for the special things in our church.
The stained-glass windows.

All
Thank you, God, we pray.

Leader
The altar.

All
Thank you, God, we pray.

Leader
The tabernacle.

All
Thank you, God, we pray.

Leader
The candles and lights.

All
Thank you, God, we pray.

Sign of the Cross

Lent

First Class/Primary Three:
Lent – Turning Time: Term 2, Lesson 4 (*Alive-O 3*, p. 195)

What am I trying to do?
As the Lenten season begins, to offer children an opportunity to explore – primarily through ritual and symbol – the experience of 'turning away' and 'turning towards', as a reflection of the Ash Wednesday call to 'Turn away from sin and embrace the Gospel'.

Why?
So that their understanding and awareness of Lent as a special liturgical season of conversion may be enhanced.

For your visit choose from the following lesson elements and suggestions:

Song
Sing or invite the children to sing *Wilderness*. Chat to them about the song.

Chatting
Chat to the children about the 'little wilderness' that they have made. This lesson helps the children to explore the liturgical season by encouraging them to reflect on 'turning away' from the busyness of their everyday lives and 'turning towards' God in thought and in prayer. The lesson introduces the children to the 'little wilderness', a place of sand and stone, as a symbol of the 'space' within which Christians are called to reflection and quiet during the season of Lent.

Chatting about Ash Wednesday: Have you ever heard of Ash Wednesday? Tell us about what you have heard.

Chatting about Lent: Have you ever heard the word 'Lent'? Where have you heard it? Tell us what you know about Lent.

Chatting about doing something for Lent: Have you ever heard someone say 'what are you doing for Lent'? What do you think this might mean? What sort of things do you think people do? Why? What do you think we could do for Lent?

Video
Watch the video piece 'Wilderness and Lent' with the children. Chat to them about what they see and hear.

Prayertime
Ash Wednesday Ritual: A priest might like to distribute the ashes to the children in class. In line with what the children are learning in school he may like to follow this Prayertime text.

Note: A child will be invited to read a short piece of text from the Bible. In preparation for this you might like to have highlighted the phrase for the child to facilitate easy reading. You might like to bring in some palm and burn a little bit of it so that the children can see where the ashes have come from.

Take the Bible from its place in the classroom.

All *(sing)*
Wilderness

Sign of the Cross

Priest
One day Jesus went into the desert.
_____ *(name reader)* will read the Word of God for us today.

The child is invited to come forward to read from the Bible.
The priest takes the Bible and ceremoniously hands it to the child.
The child faces the class, holding the Bible.

Priest
Jesus had many friends. He liked being with his friends. He liked eating with them and talking with them and sharing his life with them. Sometimes crowds of people would follow him. They wanted to hear what he had to say. They wanted to talk to him and tell him about how things were going for them. Jesus worked hard. The crowds of people often kept him busy. But he was never too busy to help those who needed him in any way.

One day Jesus decided that it would be good for him to go away and be on his own for a while. He wanted to go somewhere quiet, some place where there would be no distractions, some place where he could think and pray to God about his life, about his friends and about the world.

Then it dawned on him that the desert might be a good place for doing what he wanted to do. He went off and spent some time in the desert wilderness.

Let us listen to the Word of God as we read from the Bible.

Reader
The Lord be with you

All
And also with you.

Reader
This reading is from the Gospel according to St Mark.

All
Glory to you, O Lord.

Reader
'One day, Jesus went into the desert.'
The Gospel of the Lord *(raising Bible)*.

All
Praise to you, Lord Jesus Christ.

Priest *(holding ashes)*
Ash Wednesday is a special day. It marks the beginning of Lent.
The ashes help us to remember that it is important sometimes to turn away
from being busy, to stop and to turn towards God.

Children come forward to receive the ashes.

Priest
_____ *(name)*, turn towards God.
In the name of the Father, and of the Son and of the Holy Spirit.

Child
Amen.

When each child has received his/her ashes:

All
Turn away, turn away from too-busyness.
Be quiet, be still and pray.
Turn towards God-in-the-wilderness.
Turn, turn, day by day.

Sign of the Cross

Second Class/Primary Four:
Lent – Re-connecting: Term 2, Lesson 4 (*Alive-O 4*, p. 215)

What am I trying to do?
To offer the children an opportunity:
- to explore, through ritual and symbol, the experience of connection and disconnection as the Lenten season begins;
- to see in the Ash Wednesday invitation a call for us to re-connect with others and with God.

Why?
So that their understanding and awareness of Lent as a special liturgical season of conversion may be enhanced.

For your visit choose from the following lesson elements and suggestions:

Song
Sing or invite the children to sing *Connected*. Chat to them about the song.

Chatting
Chatting about what it feels like to be connected to others and what it feels like to be disconnected from others: What does it feel like when everyone in the class is connected to one another? What sort of things connect us to others? What does it feel like to be disconnected from others? Have you ever felt disconnected from others? Tell us about it. Who else are we connected to besides those around us? Do you think God likes being connected to us? Do you think that Lent can be a time when we remember that we are connected to others and to God? Do you think Lent is a good time to say sorry for the times when we have chosen not to be connected to those who love and care for us and have become distant from God?

Chatting about Ash Wednesday: Have you ever heard of Ash Wednesday? Tell us about what you have heard.

Chatting about doing something for Lent: Have you ever heard someone say 'what are you doing for Lent'? What do you think this might mean? What sort of things do you think people do? Why? What do you think we could do for Lent?

Pupil Book
Chat to the children about the picture and text on page 26.

Video
Watch the video piece 'Ash Wednesday', which shows the ashes being distributed.

Prayertime
Ash Wednesday Ritual: A priest might like to distribute the ashes to the children in class. In line with what the children are learning in school he may like to follow this Prayertime text.

Note: You might like to bring in some palm and burn a little of it so that the children can see where the ashes have come from.

All *(sing as priest lights candle)*
Round and round and round the earth.
Praise God, praise God.

Priest
Let us stand to hear the Word of God from the Bible.

The Lord be with you.

All
And also with you.

Priest
A reading from the holy Gospel according to Matthew *(22:37)*.

Jesus said 'You shall love the Lord your God with all your heart, and with all your soul, and with all your mind.'

The Gospel of the Lord.

All
Praise to you, Lord Jesus Christ.

Priest
We gather here today to receive ashes on our foreheads. We remember that we are connected to others. We remember that we are connected to God.

The priest invites the children to come forward for the ashes.

_____*(name)*, you are connected to God.
In the name of the Father and of the Son and of the Holy Spirit.

Child
Amen.

When the children receive the ashes they bow towards the priest and return to their place in the classroom. As the children process to the priest, the class sings quietly:

All *(sing)*
Round and round and round the earth.
Praise God, praise God.

Concluding Prayer
If possible, gather the children in a circle for the concluding prayer.

Priest
Let us stand.
Let us remember that we are all connected to one another.
Let us hold hands.
Let us remember that we all connected to the God who loves us.
Let us raise our hands together as we sing:

All *(sing)*
Connected

Sign of the Cross

Theme 6: Easter
Time of Visit: The days between Spy Wednesday and Good Friday or after the Easter holidays

Scope: All Classes

Easter is the Christian celebration of joy and new life. Resurrection is central to the Easter message. As Christians we believe that death is not the end of life but merely the beginning of a new form of life in the presence of God. Each year the children hear the Easter story. It is hoped that as they move through the primary school they will come to appreciate the centrality of the story in Christian belief and come to love and understand it more deeply as they grow older.

Alive-O begins by introducing the children in a simple way to the story of the Death and Resurrection of Jesus. The children are invited to take part in rituals that celebrate the events of the Passion, Death and Resurrection of Jesus. As the children progress through the school they come to know and appreciate the finer details and implications that surround these significant events. In all classes, however, *Alive-O* seeks to enable the children to enter fully into the Church's liturgical event at Easter and to grow in their understanding of the story of the Passion, Death and Resurrection of Jesus for themselves, for others and for the Christian community.

Junior Infants/Primary One:
Easter: Term 2, Lesson 10 (*Alive-O*, p. 185)

What am I trying to do?
To help the children to become aware that Easter is a time to celebrate because Jesus Christ is risen and is with us.

Why?
So that they will experience the joy of Easter and link their experience with our Christian belief in the Resurrection.

For your visit choose from the following lesson elements and suggestions:

Song
Sing or invite the children to sing *Alleluia*. Chat to them about the song.

Story
Read or invite the children to tell the story *An Easter Surprise*.

An Easter Surprise
Jesus was put to death on the cross. His friends took his body down from the

cross and laid it in the tomb. They left the tomb and went home. They were very sad because Jesus was no longer with them. They didn't talk or laugh or sing.

There was a woman called Mary, who was one of the friends of Jesus, who came from a place called Magdala. Mary and her friends didn't have time to finish taking care of the body of their friend Jesus. So they decided they would come back and finish their work another day. That is why, on Easter Sunday morning, they got up very, very early. They set off walking to the tomb where Jesus' body had been laid. They brought special oils and ointments and creams with them for the body.

'Oh dear,' said Mary, stopping suddenly. 'We have forgotten something.'

'What?' asked her friends.

'The huge big stone,' said Mary. 'We forgot about the huge big stone they rolled in front of the tomb where Jesus' body is.'

'That's right,' the others said. 'What shall we do?'

'We will never be able to roll it away from the entrance all by ourselves,' said Mary in a very worried voice.

'It would be much too heavy,' the others agreed.

'We will just have to think of something,' said Mary as she continued determinedly on her way.

'Perhaps there will be someone there already who will help us,' said one of the friends.

'I don't think so,' said another, 'it is much too early in the morning for anyone else to be awake.'

'We'll be okay, you'll see, we will think of something.'

But when they got to the tomb they could hardly believe their eyes. They were very surprised indeed. The huge big stone was not there! It had been rolled away. The women were very glad.

They took their oils and ointments and went inside to where the body lay. But the body was not there! Now the women were very upset.

'Where's the body of our friend Jesus?' said Mary.

'Perhaps someone has taken it away,' said the others.

'Jesus is not here, he is risen,' said a voice behind them. The women turned round and saw a young person standing there, in shining bright clothes. 'Jesus is not here, he is risen. You must go and tell everyone the good news that Jesus is risen from the dead.'

116

Mary and her friends were very happy. They ran off to tell everyone what had happened.

Chatting

Chatting about the story: Do you know anyone who died? Were you sad? Was anybody else sad? Do you think that Mary and her friends were sad because Jesus died? Do you think that they missed their friend Jesus? How do you think they felt when they heard that Jesus was not dead anymore? Do you think that this was good news? Why?

Chatting about eggs: You might like to bring an egg into class for this chatting. Chat about the fragility, shape, size and colour of the egg. What can grow inside an egg? Have you ever seen a baby chick? What does a baby chick look like? We eat eggs at Easter because we celebrate new life. What sort of eggs do you eat at Easter?

Chatting about new life: Do you remember the trees in winter – what were they like back then? When did the leaves begin to grow? Where were all the flowers like the daffodils, the snowdrops and tulips in winter? When did they begin to grow? Do you like spring? Do you think that spring is the time for new life? Why?

Chatting about the church at Easter (this chatting could take place after the Easter holidays): What does the church look like at Easter? Why do you think there are lots of flowers? What about the lights – did you see any special lights in the church at Easter? Why do you think that there are lots of lights in the church at Easter? What other times do we use candles – birthdays, weddings, Christmas time, prayertime.

Pupil Book

Chat to the children about the picture on page 34: Why are the women looking into the empty tomb? What are they saying to each other? Where do you think Mary is running off to?

Prayertime

You might like to lead the children in an Easter prayer, using the following Prayertime text.

Light the candle.

Sign of the Cross

Leader

The candle reminds us that God is with us.
It reminds us too that Jesus is not dead. He is alive.
We want to tell God that we are happy.

All (*sing*)
Alleluia

Leader
Thank you, God, for being with us always.

All
Alleluia, alleluia.

Leader
Thank you, God, for raising Jesus to new life.

All
Alleluia, alleluia.

Leader
Thank you, God, for happy times.

All
Alleluia, alleluia.
'Thank you, God, for Jesus'
Is the prayer we say.
'Thank you, God, for Jesus'
We pray on Easter day.

All (*sing*)
Alleluia

Sign of the Cross

Senior Infants/Primary Two:
Easter: Term 2, Lesson 10 (*Alive-O 2*, p. 201)

What am I trying to do?
To provide opportunities for the children to take part in simple rituals which celebrate some of the events in the stories of the Passion, Death and Resurrection of Jesus.

Why?
So that in the years to come they will be able to enter fully into the Church's liturgical events at Easter and thereby be helped to come to a deeper understanding of the story of the Passion, Death and Resurrection of Jesus.

For your visit choose from the following lesson elements and suggestions:

Song
Sing or invite the children to sing *Alleluia* or *Take and Eat*. Chat to them about the song.

Chatting
Chatting about food and eating: What are the times during the day when you usually eat your meals? What sort of food do you like? When do you eat with others at home/at school? Did Jesus eat with his friends? At Easter we remember the special meal that Jesus had with his friends on the night before he died.

Chatting about the Easter story: Do you know anyone who died? Were you sad? Was anybody else sad? Do you think that Mary and her friends were sad because Jesus died? Do you think that they missed their friend Jesus? How do you think they felt when they heard that Jesus was not dead anymore? Do you think that this was good news? Why?

Chatting about the church at Easter (this chatting could take place after the Easter holidays): What does the church look like at Easter? Why do you think there are lots of flowers? What about the lights – did you see any special lights in the church at Easter? Why do you think that there are lots of lights in the church at Easter? What other times do we use candles – birthdays, weddings, Christmas time, prayertime.

Pupil Book
Chat to the children about the picture on page 36: What is happening in the picture? How many women can you see? Can you remember their names? Why are they running? Can you see the big stone in the picture? There is a candle in the picture – what does the candle remind us of?

Video

You might like to watch the video piece 'New Life' which deals with Easter. Chat to the children about what they see and hear.

Prayertime

During the coming week up to Easter the children participate in three simple rituals centred on the Last Supper, the death of Jesus on the cross and the Resurrection. These rituals can be found in the teacher's manual. You might like to lead the children in one of these rituals. The Resurrection ritual is reproduced below.

Sign of the Cross

Leader

Today we celebrate the Resurrection of Jesus. Every Easter a special candle is lit in the church. It is called the paschal candle and it is lit to remind us that God has raised Jesus to new life. Today we light our special candle to remind us that God has raised Jesus to new life.

As we do, we pray together *(as leader lights candle)*:

All

'Thank you, God, for Jesus'
Is the prayer we say.
'Thank you, God, for Jesus'
We pray on Easter Day.

Leader

We will stand up as we listen to the story of the Resurrection.

Before we do, we will make the Sign of the Cross on our foreheads like this *(leader encourages the children to sign their foreheads as she/he does)*, on our lips like this *(leader encourages the children to sign their lips as she/he does)*, and on our hearts like this *(leader encourages the children to sign their hearts as she/he does)*.

An Easter Surprise

Jesus was put to death on the cross. His friends took his body down from the cross and laid it in the tomb. They left the tomb and went home. They were very sad because Jesus was no longer with them. They didn't talk or laugh or sing.

There was a woman called Mary, who was one of the friends of Jesus, who came from a place called Magdala. Because it was getting late, Mary and her friends didn't have time to finish taking care of the body of their friend Jesus. So they decided they would come back and finish their work another day. That is why, on Easter Sunday morning, they got up very, very early. They set off walking to the tomb where Jesus' body had been laid. They brought special oils and ointments and creams with them for the body.

'Oh dear,' said Mary, stopping suddenly. 'We have forgotten something.'

'What?' asked her friends.

'The huge big stone,' said Mary. 'We forgot about the huge big stone they rolled in front of the tomb where Jesus' body is.'

'That's right,' the others said. 'What shall we do?'

'We will never be able to roll it away from the entrance all by ourselves,' said Mary in a very worried voice.

'It would be much too heavy,' the others agreed.

'We will just have to think of something,' said Mary as she continued determinedly on her way.

'Perhaps there will be someone there already who will help us,' said one of the friends.

'I don't think so,' said another, 'it is much too early in the morning for anyone else to be awake.'

'We'll be okay, you'll see, we will think of something.'

But when they got to the tomb they could hardly believe their eyes. They were very surprised indeed. The huge big stone was not there! It had been rolled away. The women were very glad.

They took their oils and ointments and went inside to where the body lay. But the body was not there! Now the women were very upset.

'Where's the body of our friend Jesus?' said Mary.

'Perhaps someone has taken it away,' said the others.

'Jesus is not here, he is risen,' said a voice behind them. The women turned round and saw a young person standing there, in shining bright clothes. 'Jesus is not here, he is risen. You must go and tell everyone the good news that Jesus is risen from the dead.'

Mary and her friends were very happy. They ran off to tell everyone what had happened.

Leader
We sing together:

All *(sing)*
Alleluia

Leader
'Jesus is not here. He is risen.' That was the message that the women were given.

Turn to the person on either side of you and give that person the message that Jesus is risen. Tell them 'Jesus is not here. He is risen'.

(Encourage the children to spread the news.)

We sing together once again:

All *(sing)*
Alleluia

Sign of the Cross

First Class/Primary Three:
Time for Joy: Term 2, Lesson 9 (*Alive-O 3*, p. 252)

What am I trying to do?
To provide opportunities for the children to take part in a series of simple rituals that celebrate some of the events in the stories of the Passion, Death and Resurrection of Jesus.

Why?
So that they may be helped to come to a deeper understanding of the story of the Passion, Death and Resurrection of Jesus and thereby begin to learn to enter into the Church's liturgical events at Easter.

For your visit choose from the following lesson elements and suggestions:

Song
Sing or invite the children to sing *Alleluia*. Chat to them about the song.

Chatting
Chat to the children about the stories we remember during Holy Week and Easter. Invite them to tell you the story of the Last Supper.

Invite the children to tell you the story of the journey to Calvary (this year the children focus on the third, seventh, ninth and twelfth stations). Chat to them about the Stations of the Cross in the local church. Chat about the Easter story. The women share the Good News that Jesus is risen. Invite them to tell you the story.

Story
An Easter Surprise
Jesus was put to death on the cross. His friends took his body down from the cross and laid it in the tomb. They left the tomb and went home. They were very sad because Jesus was no longer with them. They didn't talk or laugh or sing.

There was a woman called Mary, who was one of the friends of Jesus, who came from a place called Magdala. Because it was getting late, Mary and her friends didn't have time to finish taking care of the body of their friend Jesus. So they decided they would come back and finish their work another day. That is why, on Easter Sunday morning, they got up very, very early. They set off walking to the tomb where Jesus' body had been laid. They brought special oils and ointments and creams with them for the body.

'Oh dear,' said Mary, stopping suddenly. 'We have forgotten something.'

'What?' asked her friends.

'The huge big stone,' said Mary. 'We forgot about the huge big stone they rolled in front of the tomb where Jesus' body is.'

'That's right,' the others said. 'What shall we do?'

'We will never be able to roll it away from the entrance all by ourselves,' said Mary in a very worried voice.

'It would be much too heavy,' the others agreed.

'We will just have to think of something,' said Mary as she continued determinedly on her way.

'Perhaps there will be someone there already who will help us,' said one of the friends.

'I don't think so,' said another, 'it is much too early in the morning for anyone else to be awake.'

'We'll be okay, you'll see, we will think of something.'

But when they got to the tomb they could hardly believe their eyes. They were very surprised indeed. The huge big stone was not there! It had been rolled away. The women were very glad.

They took their oils and ointments and went inside to where the body lay. But the body was not there! Now the women were very upset.

'Where's the body of our friend Jesus?' said Mary.

'Perhaps someone has taken it away,' said the others.

'Jesus is not here, he is risen,' said a voice behind them. The women turned round and saw a young person standing there, in shining bright clothes. 'Jesus is not here, he is risen. You must go and tell everyone the good news that Jesus is risen from the dead.'

Mary and her friends were very happy. They ran off to tell everyone what had happened.

Pupil Book
Chat to the children about the picture on page 33.

Art
If the children have made the Stations of the Cross you might like to look at them and talk to the children about what the pictures depict.

Video
You might like to watch the video piece 'Easter' with the children. This section is in three parts – Holy Thursday; Good Friday; Resurrection. Chat to

the children about what they see and hear. You might like to focus on one of the three parts.

Prayertime
This lesson provides opportunities for the children to take part in a series of simple rituals centred on the Last Supper, Good Friday and the Resurrection. These rituals can be found in the teacher's manual. The Good Friday ritual is reproduced below.

Ritual: Stations of the Cross
Note: *The children may have completed artwork on the Stations of the Cross which can be displayed in the classroom for this Prayertime.*

Sign of the Cross

All (sing)
Time and time and time again.
Praise God, praise God.

Leader
We light our candle.
God loves us and cares for us all the time.
All through his life Jesus loved those who lived and shared their life with him. He also loved God and knew that God loved him. Jesus died on the cross rather than stop loving God or his friends.

Today we will carry a crucifix and a candle and we will follow the Way of the Cross. We will remember four special moments on the journey that Jesus made on the day he died. We will remember his love for us all. We will stop four times. Each time we will say:

All (repeating after leader)
Jesus, we bless you and adore you.

Leader
Let us stand and face our first Station of the Cross: *Jesus Falls the First Time.*
We remember how Jesus carried a big heavy wooden cross all the way to the top of the hill of Calvary.

Jesus stumbles,
Falls, and then,
Stumbles on
And falls again.
Jesus on the dusty road,
Falls beneath his heavy load.

Let us pause in silence for a moment.
Let us bow our heads.
Let us pray.

All

Jesus, we bless you and adore you.

Leader

Let us turn and face our second Station of the Cross: *Jesus Falls a Second Time*. We remember how Jesus carried a big wooden cross all the way to the top of the hill of Calvary.

Jesus stumbles,
Falls, and then,
Stumbles on
And falls again.
Jesus on the dusty road,
Falls beneath his heavy load.

Let us pause in silence for a moment.
Let us bow our heads.
Let us pray.

All

Jesus, we bless you and adore you.

Leader

Let us turn and face our third Station of the Cross: *Jesus Falls a Third Time*. We remember how Jesus carried a big wooden cross all the way to the top of the hill of Calvary.

Jesus stumbles,
Falls, and then,
Stumbles on
And falls again.
Jesus on the dusty road,
Falls beneath his heavy load.

Let us pause in silence for a moment.
Let us bow our heads.
Let us pray.

All

Jesus, we bless you and adore you.

Leader

Let us turn and face our fourth Station of the Cross: *Jesus Dies on the Cross*. We remember how Jesus died on the cross. We remember how Mary, his mother, and John, his friend, stood by.

Mary stands
That dreadful day,
Friends and comrades

Ran away.
Only John remains to cry,
Only one to say goodbye.

Soldiers ask
'Why did he die?'
Loving Son
Of God most high.
Loving people great and small,
Giving up his life for all.

Let us pause in silence for a moment.
Let us bow our heads.
Let us pray.

All
Jesus, we bless you and adore you.

Leader *(placing crucifix and lighted candle on the table)*
Let us stand. God sent Jesus into the world. Most clearly of all, Jesus shows us how much God loves us and cares for us. We give thanks to God.

All *(sing)*
Time and time and time again.
Praise God, praise God.

Sign of the Cross

Second Class/Primary Four:
The Passion and Death of Jesus: Term 2, Lesson 9
(*Alive-O 4*, p. 283)

What am I trying to do?
To provide opportunities for the children to take part in a series of simple rituals which celebrate some of the events in the stories of the Passion, Death and Resurrection of Jesus.

Why?
So that they may be helped to come to a deeper understanding of the story of the Passion, Death and Resurrection of Jesus and thereby begin to enter more fully into the Church's liturgical events at Easter.

The Resurrection: Term 2, Lesson 10 (*Alive-O 4*, p. 294)

What am I trying to do?
To continue to introduce the children to the apostles' experience of the Risen Jesus as told in the New Testament apparition narratives.

Why?
So that the children may:
*   be able to recognise the Risen Jesus in their own lives;
*   become aware of the continuing presence and action of the Risen Jesus in their own lives and in the Christian community;
*   be better able to enter into the Church's liturgical celebrations at Easter.

For your visit choose from the following lesson elements and suggestions:

Song
Sing or invite the children to sing *Stabat Mater* or *Peter Remembers or Alleluia*. Chat to them about the song.

Story
Read/tell or invite the children to tell one of the following stories: *The Last Supper, The Crucifixion* or *Follow Me.*

The Last Supper
(Adapted from Luke 22:7-20)

On the first day of the Passover celebration, Jesus, his friends and his followers discussed the preparations they would have to make for the Passover meal. Jesus sent some of them to a house that he knew in the city of Jerusalem. There they would prepare a big room and food for the meal. They were very busy. They set out the room. They had to get some herbs and a one-year-old lamb. They had to make some unleavened bread and buy some red wine. When Jesus and the others arrived, everything was ready.

When evening came, everyone sat down to eat the Passover meal. They said special prayers, they shared their special story about Moses leading the people out of Egypt, and they shared their special memory of things that had happened to their people in times past. This Passover was the same as every other Passover until, as they were sharing the special food and wine, Jesus did something that was very different to every other Passover. He took the unleavened bread and blessed it and broke it and shared it out among his friends and followers, and he said, 'This is my body, take and eat it.' Then he took the cup of wine. He blessed it and said, 'This is my blood, take and drink it.'

Jesus' friends and followers had never seen this done, or heard these words spoken, at a Passover meal before. This was new. At first they weren't sure what Jesus meant, but he said to them, 'Do this in memory of me.'

When the supper was over, Jesus and his friends went off to the Garden of Gethsemene to pray.

The Crucifixion
(Adapted from Luke 23)

It was Passover time. Jesus and many of his disciples went to Jerusalem to retell the story of Moses and his people and to eat the Passover meal. Afterwards, Jesus and a few of his close friends went to a garden on the hill of Gethsemene to pray.

Jesus was afraid that those people who did not want to hear what he taught them, also wanted to get rid of him. They were envious of the way crowds of people followed Jesus, feasting on his every word. He prayed to the Father to help him and give him the strength and courage to live out his life to the end, still showing the people God's love. God heard his prayer and gave him the strength he needed.

As he knelt praying, Roman soldiers burst into the garden. They grabbed Jesus and took him away. They brought him to Pilate, the Roman governor. Pilate asked Jesus what he had done wrong, why these people wanted to get rid of him, but Jesus said that he had done nothing. Pilate didn't think Jesus had done anything wrong, but he did not want to upset the leaders of the Temple who had ordered that Jesus be brought to him. He offered the people a choice – he would release Jesus or another prisoner, called Barabbas, who was a criminal. Stirred by the leaders of the Temple, the people chose Barabbas. He was released and Jesus was led away, to be tortured. When he was bruised and covered in blood, Pilate had him brought back to the people, thinking that they might feel sorry for him. But they shouted aloud, 'Crucify him, Crucify him.' Finally, Pilate gave in and Jesus was led to the foot of the hill of Calvary. A crown of thorns was placed on his head. People mocked and called him 'King of the Jews'. He was given a heavy wooden cross and ordered to climb to the top of the hill. As he climbed, Jesus grew weaker and weaker, falling three times. A man called Simon of Cyrene helped him to carry the cross and became a friend of Jesus.

At the top of the hill, soldiers nailed Jesus to the cross. Two other criminals were crucified at the same time, one on Jesus' right and the other on his left. Jesus prayed to God, asking him to forgive them for whatever wrong they had done. One criminal thanked Jesus. Jesus promised him, 'Today you will be with me in the Father's kingdom.'

Jesus hung on the cross for three hours. His close friends and his mother stood at the foot of the cross, comforting him. His strength began to fail and he whispered a final prayer to the Father, 'Father, into your hands I place my life.' Then, Jesus bowed his head and died.

Jesus' friends took his body down from the cross and wrapped it in clean linen.

Follow Me
(Adapted from John 21)

One day, sometime after Jesus' death, Simon Peter and some of the apostles and friends of Jesus were sitting by the Sea of Tiberius. They were quiet, each one thinking different thoughts and remembering different things that had happened when Jesus was with them.

Simon Peter remembered the day by the well outside the town of Samaria when Jesus asked a woman to give him a drink of water.

John was thinking about the day on the hillside when Jesus had blessed the bread and broken it and shared it out among the hungry crowd, who ate heartily and happily.

Andrew was preoccupied with recent stories he had heard of disciples claiming that they had seen Jesus, that they had spoken to him, that he was no longer dead but had risen. Andrew didn't quite know what to make of these stories. 'But,' he said, bemused, 'Jesus himself told stories and I wasn't sure what to make of those either!' He remembered the story about the sower and the seed; the one about the woman and the lost coin, and the one about the lamp with the bowl over its head.

Suddenly, as though he remembered another day when he and his brother Andrew had left their nets to follow Jesus, Simon Peter jumped to his feet. 'I am a fisherman,' he announced, 'I'm going fishing!'

He ran to the edge of the water. The others followed him. They climbed into a boat and rowed out onto the lake. They spent the night fishing, but caught nothing. When morning came, a man who was walking on the shore called to them, 'Have you caught anything, friends?'

'Not a thing,' Simon Peter shouted back.

'Throw the net out to starboard and you'll catch something,' the man called out. The disciples were all very tired by now, but the man spoke with authority so, reluctantly, they did as he said. To their amazement they caught such a huge haul of fish that they had difficulty rowing the boat back to the shore. This was the kind of haul they had dreamed about catching. As they hauled in the nets they began to realise who had called to them. It must be Jesus; they were sure it was Jesus – yet they did not want to ask.

They came ashore to the welcome sight of a cheery fire and the smell of fish cooking. There was bread to eat as well. 'Bring some of the fish you have caught and come and have some breakfast,' Jesus invited.

When everyone had gathered round, Jesus took the bread in his hands. He broke it and shared it out among them. He did the same with the fish. It was just like old times. They were hungry, he fed them. They ate what he shared with them and listened to what he said, feasting on every word.

When everyone had finished eating, the Risen Jesus spoke to Simon Peter. 'Follow me,' he said.

Chatting
Chatting about the stories: The Last Supper: Did Jesus often have meals with his friends? Tell us some stories of when Jesus ate with his friends? What happened at the Last Supper? What story were Jesus' friends remembering and celebrating? What did Jesus say during the Last Supper? *The Crucifixion:* Why did Jesus go to the Garden of Gethsemane to pray? Did God the Father listen to Jesus pray? Who was Pilate? Who helped Jesus carry his cross? *Follow Me:* Why were the apostles sad? What happened when they were fishing? Do you think they found it easy or difficult to recognise the Risen Jesus?

Pupil Book
Chat to the children about the pictures and text on pages 30, 31 and 32.

Art
In these lessons the children have had an opportunity to draw the Stations of the Cross, to make a cross and to make a Resurrection (Zig-zag) Card. If the children have become involved in the art work you might like to ask them to show their work to you. Chat to them about what they have done.

Video
Watch the video piece 'The Passion and Death of Jesus' on the theme of Holy Week. Chat to the children about what they see and hear.

Prayertime
During the weeks coming up to Easter the children participate in a series of classroom rituals centred on the Last Supper, the Stations of the Cross and the Resurrection. These can be found in the teacher's manual. A Prayertime on the Resurrection is reproduced below.

Sign of the Cross

Leader *(as the candle is lit)*
Jesus is risen.
Alleluia, Alleluia!

The Risen Jesus was with the disciples. They were filled with joy when they realised that he was alive. The Risen Jesus is alive today and with us. Let us be full of joy as we say together:

All *(repeating after leader)*
The Risen Jesus is alive and with us.

Leader
He is with us each and every day.

All
The Risen Jesus is alive and with us.

Leader
He is with us when we play.

All
The Risen Jesus is alive and with us.

Leader
He is with us when we work.

All
The Risen Jesus is alive and with us.

Leader
He is with us at home among those whom we love.

All
The Risen Jesus is alive and with us.

Leader
He is with us at school as we learn.

All
The Risen Jesus is alive and with us.

Leader
He is with us as we gather together at Mass.

All
The Risen Jesus is alive and with us.

Leader
May we, like the disciples, recognise that the Lord Jesus is with us always. Let us sing:

All *(sing)*
Alleluia

Sign of the Cross

Theme 7: Mary
Time of Visit: First Week of May

Scope: All Classes

Mary has always been honoured within the Catholic tradition. We honour her as the mother of Jesus. Advent and Christmas and the months of October are special times of devotion to Mary. Mary is a figure of faith and discipleship. She is someone who embraced the joy of the birth of her son, Jesus, and the sorrow of his trial and suffering when she watched him die. Her compassion, her strength in adversity, her open heart and her dedicated love of God have inspired countless generations.

Alive-O honours Mary as the mother of God's son Jesus and as our mother too. Junior Infants/Primary One hear the story of Mary as she rejoices in the birth of her son, Jesus. Senior Infants/Primary Two (*Alive-O 2*) have an opportunity to participate in a Prayer Service around the May altar, while First Class/Primary Three (*Alive-O 3*) and Second Class/Primary Four (*Alive-O 4*) recall the significant moments in Mary's life and are introduced to the Rosary.

Junior Infants/Primary One:
Mary and Joseph Wait: Term 1, Lesson 14 (*Alive-O*, p. 102)

What am I trying to do?
To help the children to recognise that there are different kinds of waiting; specifically to help them to be aware of the kind of waiting that is hopeful. To introduce children to the story of the journey of Mary and Joseph from Nazareth to Bethlehem.

Why?
So that they will reflect on their own experience of waiting for Christmas.

For your visit choose from the following lesson elements and suggestions:

Story
Recall with the children the stories about Mary: *Mary and Joseph go on a Journey* and *The Waiting is Over.* (See pp. 60 and 82 of this book.)

Chatting
Chat to the children about the sort of person/mother Mary was. What was Mary like? What sort of things does your mother (or whoever looks after you) do for you? What sort of things do you think Mary did for Jesus?

Prayertime
You might like to do the following Prayertime with the children. It honours mums/dads/those who love us.

Sign of the Cross

The candle is lit.

Leader
Today we ask God to bless us and to bless our friends and families.

Bless our mums.

All
God, bless us and keep us, we pray.
God, bless us and keep us, each day.

Leader
Bless our dads.

All
God, bless us and keep us, we pray.
God, bless us and keep us, each day.

Leader
Bless our brothers.

All
God, bless us and keep us, we pray.
God, bless us and keep us, each day.

Leader
Bless our sisters.

All
God, bless us and keep us, we pray.
God, bless us and keep us, each day.

Leader
Bless the friends we play with at home.

All
God, bless us and keep us, we pray.
God, bless us and keep us, each day.

Leader
Bless the friends we play with in school.

All
God, bless us and keep us, we pray.
God, bless us and keep us, each day.

Leader

Bless all those who live near us.

All

God, bless us and keep us, we pray.
God, bless us and keep us, each day.

Hail Mary, full of grace,
The Lord is with thee.
Blessed art thou among women
And blessed is the fruit of thy womb, Jesus.
Holy Mary, mother of God,
Pray for us sinners,
Now, and at the hour of our death. Amen.

Sign of the Cross

Senior Infants/Primary Two:
I Want a Word: Term 3, Lesson 4 (*Alive-O 2*, p. 230)

What am I trying to do?
To provide an opportunity for the children to celebrate their use of words.
To provide an opportunity for the parents, parish personnel, teacher and children to honour Mary, the Mother of Jesus.

Why?
So that they will have some concept of the power of the word and be able to appreciate the importance of God's Word.

For your visit choose from the following lesson elements and suggestions:

Chatting
Chatting about Mary: What stories do you know about Mary? What do you think she was like? Would you like to have Mary as your mother? Why? What sort of things do mothers (or people who love us) do for us? What sort of things did Mary do for Jesus?

Chatting about the May altar: What is a May altar? Why is May a special month? Did you ever make a May altar at home? Tell us about a time someone at home made a May altar.

Prayertime
At the end of this lesson the children are invited to partake along with their parents/guardians in a Prayer Service around the May altar. You might like to lead the children and their parents/guardians in the Prayer Service, using the following text.

Sign of the Cross

Leader
Welcome to our Prayer Service to celebrate Mary's month, the month of May, and to ask Mary for her help every day. We begin by singing the hymn that tells us what God asked of Mary. God asked Mary to be the mother of Jesus.

All *(sing)*
Mary

Leader
Mary did what God asked of her. God was pleased with Mary. We now ask Mary to help us to do what God wants us to do. We ask her to help us to grow in God's love as Jesus grew in God's love. We pray:

Child 1
Help us, Mary, to be kind and gentle.

All
Hail Mary, full of grace.

Child 2
Help us, Mary, to be caring at home.

All
Hail Mary, full of grace.

Child 3
Help us, Mary, to be caring in school.

All
Hail Mary, full of grace.

Child 4
Help us, Mary, to be caring when we play together.

All
Hail Mary, full of grace.

Child 5
Help us, Mary, to remember to take special care of children who are younger than ourselves.

All
Hail Mary, full of grace.

Child 6
Help us, Mary, to remember to care for the trees and plants and all of the world of nature.

All
Hail Mary, full of grace.

Leader
Let us pray together:

All
Hail Mary, full of grace,
The Lord is with thee.
Blessed art thou among women
And blessed is the fruit of thy womb, Jesus.
Holy Mary, mother of God,
Pray for us sinners,
Now, and at the hour of our death. Amen.

Leader
During the week you have been thinking and chatting about all the different kinds of words in the world.

Loud words like...
(Encourage the children to make suggestions.)
Soft words like...
(Encourage the children to make suggestions.)
Fun words like...
(Encourage the children to make suggestions.)
Words of love like...
(Encourage the children to make suggestions.)
Then there are God's words. God's word is in a special book, the Bible. Today we will listen to some of God's words from the Bible. Let's get ready to hear God's word. Let's stand up.

(Leader goes towards the Bible and raises it in both hands.)

An angel came to Mary and said: 'God is pleased with you. You are going to have a baby – a very special baby. You will call him Jesus.' Mary said, 'I will do whatever God wants me to.' *(Luke 1:30)*

Let's say thanks to God.

All
Thanks be to God.

Leader
Now let us bring forward our flowers and our pictures of flowers. Flowers have no words, but they do say something. Flowers can say 'thank you'. They can say 'well done'. They can say 'get well'. We give our flowers to Mary now to say 'we love you and we honour you'.

You might like to invite a parent/guardian to read the reflection on page 237 of Alive-O 2.

Leader
Before we go let's say, once again, our prayer to Mary.

All
Hail Mary, full of grace,
The Lord is with thee.
Blessed art thou among women
And blessed is the fruit of thy womb, Jesus.
Holy Mary, mother of God,
Pray for us sinners,
Now, and at the hour of our death. Amen.

Leader
Let's ask God to bless us.

All
God bless us and keep us, we pray.
God bless us and keep us each day. Amen.

First Class/Primary Three:
Mary's Joy: Term 3, Lesson 1 (*Alive-O 3*, p. 262)

What am I trying to do?
To introduce the children to the Joyful Mysteries of the Rosary and to encourage in them a devotion to Mary.

Why?
So that the children may honour Mary as the mother of God's son, and as our mother too.

For your visit choose from the following lesson elements and suggestions:

Song
Invite the children to sing *Mary, Our Mother*. Chat to them about the song.

Story
The children by this time have heard the following stories about Mary: *One Moment* (The Annunciation), *Two Cousins* (The Visitation), *The Moment They'd All Been Waiting For* (The Birth of Jesus), *Jesus goes to Jerusalem* (The Finding of the Child Jesus in the Temple).

Chatting
Chatting about Mary: What was the mother of Jesus called? What do you think she was like? What sort of things would she have done all day? What times of the year do we hear about Mary? Do you know any story about Mary? What is the special prayer to Mary called?

Chatting about the May altar: What is a May altar? Have you ever made one? How would you make a May altar? Why do we have May altars?

Chat about the stories the children have heard about Mary.

Pupil Book
Chat to the children about the pictures on pages 34, 35, 36 and 37. You might like to talk to the children about the Joyful Mysteries of the Rosary by using the pictures in the pupil book to recall the stories.

Art
The children have had the opportunity to make a card to Mary and a simple form of a Rosary beads. If they have completed this activity you might like to talk to them about the card and the beads that they have made.

Video
Watch the video piece 'Mary' with the class. Chat to the children about what they see and hear.

Prayertime
You might like to lead the children in a decade of the Rosary.

Second Class/Primary Four:
Mary Our Mother: Term 3, Lesson 1 (*Alive-O 4*, p. 305)

What am I trying to do?
To introduce the children to the Sorrowful Mysteries of the Rosary and to encourage in them a devotion to Mary.

Why?
So that they may honour Mary as the mother of God's son, and as our mother too.

For your visit choose from the following lesson elements and suggestions:

Song
Invite the children to sing *Stabat Mater* or *Mary Our Mother.* Chat to them about the song.

Story
Read or ask the children to tell the story *Mary Remembers.*

Mary Remembers
When Jesus had been taken down from the cross and laid in the tomb, his friends took Mary, his mother, home. She was very tired. Her friends told her to try to get some rest. But she could not rest; she could not sleep. She kept thinking back over what had happened to her son.

She remembered what Peter had told her – how Jesus had been very afraid and how he had gone to the Garden of Gethsemene to pray to the Father to help him and be with him, to give him strength and courage.

She remembered how the soldiers had tied her son to a pillar and beaten him.

She remembered the crown of thorns they had placed on his head while they mocked him and called him 'King of the Jews'.

She remembered the huge heavy cross they had placed on his shoulders and forced him to carry all the way up the hill. She remembered how he had fallen three times under the weight of the cross.

She remembered his body, hanging on that cross, until eventually his strength and his breath gave up and he died.

Mary said to herself, 'I will remember these as the five most sorrowful moments in my life.'

Chatting

Chatting about Mary: Let's see what we know about Mary... (Gradually build up a short fact file about Mary with the children.)

Chatting about the May altar: What is a May altar? Have you ever made one? How would you make a May altar? Why do we have May altars?

Chatting about the Rosary: Does anyone know what the special prayers to Mary are? Have you ever said the Rosary? Tell us about it. Have you ever heard other people say the Rosary? Do you have a Rosary beads? Do you know anyone who has a Rosary beads? You might like to show the children a Rosary beads and chat with them about how we pray with the beads.

Chat to the children about the stories that make up the Sorrowful Mysteries of the Rosary.

Pupil Book

Chat to the children about the picture and text on page 33. Read the poem and chat to them about it.

Art

In this lesson the children have the opportunity to make flowers in honour of Mary. If the children have made the flowers, you might like to look at them and to talk about them with the children.

Prayertime

You might like to lead the children in a decade of the Rosary or follow the Prayertime as outlined below.

Sign of the Cross

All *(sing)*
Mary Our Mother

Leader *(as the candle is lit)*
Mother of Jesus, blessed are you.
Mother of Jesus, my mother too.
Help me to live like Jesus
And help me to live like you.

Today let us pray the Fourth Sorrowful Mystery – The Carrying of the Cross.

You might like to invite a child or a group in the class to lead the Rosary.

As we pray the Rosary we remember how Mary felt as she watched Jesus carry his cross to Calvary. We ask her to be with us when we find things difficult.

Child/Group/Leader

Our Father, who art in heaven
Hallowed be thy name.
Thy kingdom come,
Thy will be done on earth as it is in heaven.

Class

Give us this day our daily bread
And forgive us our trespasses
As we forgive those who trespass against us.
And lead us not into temptation
But deliver us from evil. Amen.

Child/Group/Leader

Hail Mary, full of grace,
The Lord is with thee.
Blessed art thou among women
And blessed is the fruit of thy womb, Jesus.

Class

Holy Mary, Mother of God,
Pray for us sinners,
Now, and at the hour of our death. Amen.

(Repeat ten times in all)

Child/Group/Leader

Glory be to the Father,
And to the Son,
And to the Holy Spirit.

Class

As it was in the beginning,
Is now and ever shall be,
World without end. Amen.

Sign of the Cross

Theme 8: End-of-Year Celebrations
Time of Visit: Last week of the school year

Scope: All Classes

At the end of each year the children have the opportunity to reflect on all they have learnt during the school year. They do this reflection through song, music, game, story and prayer. The end-of-year celebrations can offer the visitor to the classroom a wonderful opportunity to rejoice with the children on the safe completion of the school year and to pray with them as they begin the summer holidays.

Some classes may put on a 'concert'. The concert helps to affirm the children in their learning and in their growth during the year. All classes present the children with an end-of-year *Alive-O* certificate.

Junior Infants/Primary One: Term 3, Lesson 7 (*Alive-O*, p. 240)

Senior Infants/Primary Two: Term 3, Lesson 7 (*Alive-O 2*, p. 256)

First Class/Primary Three: Term 3, Lesson 8 (*Alive-O 3*, p. 340)

Second Class/Primary Four: Term 3, Lesson 11 (*Alive-O 4*, p. 421)

For your visit choose from the following lesson elements and suggestions:

Song
Invite the children to sing *Alive-O*. Chat to them about the song.

Chatting
Chat to the children about their favourites stories. You might let them know what your favourites are!

Chat to them about their favourite songs. Invite them to sing their favourites!

Chat to them about their favourite memories of the year.

Art
During this lesson each class will prepare for the celebration at the end of the week. You might like to ask the children to show you how they are preparing for the celebration through artwork.

Video
The final section of the video in most programmes marks the end of the school year: *Alive-O:* 'Food/Summer is Here'; *Alive-O 2:* 'Hurray for Summer';

Alive-O 3: 'Celebration'; *Alive-O 4:* 'Celebrating *Alive-O*'. You might like to watch the video with the children and join in the songs and celebration.

Prayertime

You might like to join with the children in their end-of-year prayer. Each year has its own individual end-of-year Prayertime which can be found in the teacher's manual. The Prayertime from *Alive-O 3* is reproduced below.

Celebratory Ritual

Sign of the Cross

All *(sing)*
Together Again/Alive-O

Leader
Today is a special day. Today is our last day in this class. We have been together all year long. Maybe we are excited to know that the summer holidays are here. Maybe we feel sad because some of us will be saying goodbye to each other for a while. But it is now time to move on.

Let us light our candle.

Let us ask God to be with us as we move on.

All
God be with us on our way.

Leader
As we say goodbye to this class.

All
God be with us on our way.

Leader
As we say goodbye to each other.

All
God be with us on our way.

Leader
As we begin our summer holidays.

All
God be with us on our way.

Leader
We have had a good year together.
Let us thank God now for all that we have learned.

For songs to sing. Let us sing a favourite song now.

146

All
Song of children's choice
Thank you, God, for the songs to sing.

Leader
For stories/poems to tell. Let us tell a story/poem now.

All
Story/poem of children's choice
Thank you, God, for the stories/poems to tell.

Leader
For games to play. Let us play a game now.

All
Game of children's choice
Thank you, God, for the games to play.

Leader
Thank you, God, for everything that we learned this year.
Thank you for the gift of each other.

The leader presents the Certificate of Belonging to each child as the rest of the class applauds.

Leader
May God bless us and keep us safe.

All
Amen.

Leader
May God bless our families and friends.

All
Amen.

Leader
May God bless each and everyone as we make the Sign of the Cross.

All
In the name of the Father,
And of the Son,
And of the Holy Spirit.
Amen.

All *(sing)*
Alive-O

Sign of the Cross

Section Three: Saints Alive-O!

Children love stories. They will listen to the same story over and over. Story-telling as an art form is an integral part of the Christian tradition.

Each year *Alive-O* introduces the children to the story of an Irish saint. Junior Infants/Primary One learn about Saint Brigid – a woman of extraordinary courage and wisdom whose love for God was reflected in her passion to work for justice and in her deep compassion for animals and people in need. The following year in Senior Infants/Primary Two (*Alive-O 2*) the children hear about Saint Patrick as a man who possessed a keen awareness of God's presence in all life and a deep desire to bring others to the same awareness. *Alive-O 3* and *Alive-O 4* (First and Second Class/Primary Three and Primary Four) present the lives of Columba (Colmcille) and Gobnait.

You might like to organise your visit to coincide with the time of the year when the children are hearing about the saints. The following grid outlines the time these lessons occur during the school year.

Saint	Programme	Time of Year	Term
Brigid	*Alive-O*, p. 132 Junior Infants/Primary One	Spring	Two
	Alive-O 2, p. 149 Senior Infants/Primary Two	Spring	Two
Patrick	*Alive-O 2*, p. 182 Senior Infants/Primary Two	Spring	Two
Columba	*Alive-O 3*, p. 55 First Class/Primary Three	Autumn	One
Gobnait	*Alive-O 4*, p. 408 Second Class/Primary Four	Summer	Three

If you choose to take the life of one of the saints as the focus of your visit, you might find the following suggestions useful.

Song

Invite the children to sing the song they have learnt about the specific saint.

We Sing a Song to Brigid (*Alive-O*, p. 138)
Saint Patrick's Song (*Alive-O 2*, p. 186)
Columba (*Alive-O 3*, p. 63)
Litany of the Saints (*Gobnait*) (*Alive-O 4*, p. 420)

148

Story

Read or invite the children to tell the story(ies) of the saint's lives.

Saint Brigid and the Butter (Alive-O: Junior Infants/Primary One)
(In telling this story, you may like to substitute the word 'tub' for the word 'pat';
and 'bowl' instead of 'churn'. Alternatively you might like to say a simple word or
two about how people used to make their own butter in the old days. It didn't come
in tubs like we have today, but in butter pats. It was made in a very big bowl, called
a churn.)

Like all saints, Brigid was a very good and kind person. She was especially kind and good to poor people because she understood that God has a special love for them too.

One day an old woman heard about Brigid. She went to Brigid's house. Brigid was making butter in her churn. But she did not have very much milk – only enough to make one small pat of butter. As Brigid was working away, the old woman knocked on the door. She was very poor and very hungry.

'Oh dear, oh dear. What am I to do!' she whined. 'I have not eaten these three days. I cannot go one step further unless I get something to eat.' Brigid was very sorry for the old woman. She looked all around to see what she could give her, but all she had was one small pat of butter. 'We haven't even enough butter here for ourselves,' she said, looking at the little pat, 'but this old woman is much more hungry than we are. She must have our butter.' And Brigid gave it to her.

When the old woman saw what Brigid did, she realised that Brigid must be a very special person indeed and that God must be very close to her. Brigid often gave away food to those who were poor and hungry. The people loved Brigid for her kindness.

Saint Brigid Builds her Church (Alive-O: Junior Infants/Primary One;
Alive-O 2: Senior Infants/Primary Two)
Brigid and her friends wanted to tell all the people in the land about the love of God. They wanted everyone to hear the Good News that God loved them. Brigid decided she must build a church, so that everyone would have a place to come when they wanted to talk to God.

But Brigid had no land to build her church on.

'Someone will have to give me land on which to build my church,' she said to her friends. 'I will go to the chieftain and ask him for a piece of ground.' And off she went.

Now the chieftain was a very sly man. He did not know anything about God's love and he did not want to listen to Brigid. He decided he would play a trick on her.

When Brigid asked the chieftain for some land on which to build her church, he said, 'Very well. Come with me.' He took Brigid to the top of a high hill. 'Look down there,' he said. 'All the land, as far as you can see, is mine. It belongs to me.'

Then he told Brigid to take off her cloak.

'You asked me for land,' he said. 'I will give you as much land as your cloak can cover. Take it off and lay it down on the ground and see how much ground it covers.'

Brigid was very disappointed. She knew her cloak was very small and would not cover nearly enough land to build a church. The chieftain laughed and laughed.

Brigid laid her cloak on the ground. You would hardly believe what happened next. The cloak began to grow bigger and bigger. It spread out wider and wider, further and further. The chieftain stopped laughing. His face grew pale. The cloak was still growing.

'Stop it!' cried the chieftain. 'Stop it, please! Stop it quickly! Stop it now!'

Now it was Brigid's turn to laugh. She told the cloak to stop. She had more than enough land now to build her church. She went back and told her friends what had happened. That night they thanked God for helping them with their church.
> *Patricia Egan*

Saint Patrick's Fire *(Alive-O 2: Senior Infants/Primary Two)*
The High King of Ireland was the most powerful person in the land. His name was Laoire. He lived on the Hill of Tara. From there he could see the countryside for miles and miles around.

Every year, when winter was over, and spring was about to arrive, King Laoire would light a huge bonfire – the biggest bonfire in the land – on top of the Hill of Tara. When people saw its light, in the darkness of the night, they knew that winter was over. They knew that the long nights were over. They knew that spring had come.

King Laoire had a rule, a very important rule. He ordered that no one in the land was allowed to light a bonfire before him. He ordered that his huge bonfire must be the first to be lit. Anyone who lit a bonfire before him would be punished.

There was another high hill in Ireland. It was called the Hill of Slane. Saint Patrick lived for a time on the Hill of Slane. Patrick built a bonfire there. The people asked him why he was building a bonfire. He told them that when people would see the light of his bonfire, in the dark, it would help them to know that God was with them always. Just as we remember when we light our candle at Prayertime that God is always with us, Patrick's fire would remind the people that God was with them. They would know that God would light up the darkness for them and give them life and love. Patrick told them that his fire was different to King Laoire's.

When the time came for King Laoire to light his fire, Patrick was ready. Patrick lit his fire first. It flamed and blazed and burned through the darkness. Far away on the Hill of Tara, the High King saw Patrick's fire. He was very angry. He wanted to know who had dared to disobey his rule. When he heard that it was Patrick, he gathered his soldiers together and rode off to the Hill of Slane where Patrick was.

Patrick was not afraid of King Laoire. He looked him straight in the eye.

'Why have you disobeyed me?' the King shouted.

'My fire is different to your fire,' answered Patrick. He told the King about his fire and about God's love and how God brings light to those in darkness. The King had never heard a story like this before. He was not angry anymore. From that day on he became one of Saint Patrick's friends.

Columba *(Alive-O 3: First Class/Primary Three)*
Most stories begin with beginnings,
    This story begins with the end,
Of an old man's life on an island
    And a horse's goodbye to his friend.

One Saturday morning Columba
    Woke up in bed and just knew
That this, the last day of the week,
    Was going to be his last day too.

He jumped out of bed, determined,
    It being the day that was in it,
To continue his life as he had always done,
    Living, to the very last minute.

Resting his head in his hands he prayed,
    *¹'Buíochas le Dia go deo!
Molaimid thú, móraimid thú
    Thall 's abhus 's anseo.'

Patting the pillow, 'Goodbye Bed,' he said,
    'In you I have known rest 'n peace,
No matter how dark or dreary the night
    You cradled me, *²'rís 's arís.

Goodbye Window,' he said, opening it wide,
    'You brought fresh air and light to my life.
You helped me breathe; you helped me see
    Through troubles and struggles and strife.

Goodbye Room,' he said, as he closed the door,
    'You gave me space – just to *be*
On my own, with you, when I needed –
    Just the two of us; you Room, and me.'

Neither Bed, Window nor Room
    Moved or uttered a word,
But the old saint knew, as old saints do,
    That each one had listened and heard.

It was May, the first month of summer,
    Columba's last of the year.
His friends were at work in the western fields,
    They stopped as the old man drew near.

'I have this notion,' Columba said,
    'Don't ask me how, what or why,
But I know in my heart, I feel in my bones,
    It's time, time for goodbye.'

'Where are you going?' they asked in alarm.
    'I'm going away,' he replied,
'I won't be back, but I'll see you again,
    If you know what I mean,' he smiled.

That said, he opened the doors of the barn
    And blessed its stores of grain.
*³'*Tá Dia maith*, you'll not want for food
    When I'm gone,' he repeated again.

Tired, though not yet quite finished,
    Columba sat down for a rest
On an old millstone by the side of the road.
    'Brother Diarmuid,' he said, 'Have you guessed?'

'Guessed what, Brother?' Diarmuid his friend asked,
    'I feel cross, yet I'm sad deep inside.
You talk of goodbye, of going away.
    What is it you're trying to hide?'

Just at that moment a *⁴*sean-chapall bán*
    With head drooping low in dismay,
Plodded along towards Columba, and stood
    Bereft of a whinney, or neigh.

Silent, he stood there, his mild mannered eyes
    Filled with sorrow intense.
He knew his old friend was going to die,
    Though how he knew – that baffles sense!

'Goodbye my sean-chapall,' Columba said,
    'Surefooted, dependable friend.
On the broad of your back you carried me,
    *⁵*Beannacht Dé leat*. Amen.'

He stroked the old horse's forehead,
    Its eyes filled with tears to the brim.
They spilled over, rolled down its cheeks,
    And dropped from its quivering chin.

'Your tears are upsetting Columba,
    Go away horse,' Diarmuid protested.
'Let him be!' said Columba, 'this dumb creature knew,
    Though you have not even guessed it.

He senses that I am dying.
    I tell you, else you wouldn't know,
This creature's natural horse-sense
    Is a wonder God has bestowed.'

A last look to Ireland, then back to Iona,
    Where he had come to reside.
As the Sean-chapall turned and ambled away,
    Columba lay down – and died.

Columba just lay down and died
    At rest in peace. Amen.
Now this story has reached its beginning
    Because death is never the end.

Footnotes

*¹	Glory to God above.		*³	God is good
	We praise you. We bless you, we thank you.		*⁴	Old White Horse
	We live out each day in your love.		*⁵	God bless you
*²	Again and again			

Thanks 'Bee' To God *(Alive-O 4: Second Class/Primary Four)*
Listen! Come quick till you hear.
You'll never believe – but it's true.
I saw it myself with my very own eyes.
It happened! It did! I'm telling you!

There we were, Muintir Baile Mhuirne,[1]
Not a care in the world, not a bother
Except for the usual worries 'bout – oh…
This, that and the other.

Next thing, out of nowhere, a terrible screech –
'He's coming! *An Creachaire Crua!*[2]
It's the Cattle Raider; he's on the rampage!
Send for the *Beachaire Rua!*'[3]

Pandemonium reigned, the people cried,
'A Bheachaire Rua, please, please…'
(By the way, you do know the Beachaire Rua?
It's Gobnait, the saint who keeps bees.)

'Gobnait, he's coming… he's coming…
Can't you hear the rumble of feet?
It's his army trampling all over
Our plots of oats and wheat.'

Despite all the panic around her,
Despite all the clamour and din,
Gobnait (like all wise bee-keepers)
Remained calm and quiet within.

From over the hill a yowl exploded
Like a thunder-clap, splitting a rock;
The Creachaire roared, his army advanced,
Rounding up cattle and stock.

'Gobnait, *a chara,*[4] please help us.
Without cattle we've no milk, no bread,
No butter, no meat, nothing to trade,
And how will our children be fed?'

Gobnait looked at their faces,
The faces of neighbours and friends.
'You are my people, I love you.
We have trouble. Let us pray.' Then…

From the quiet and stillness inside her
Saint Gobnait began to pray.
The bees in the hive heard her voice
And 'hummed' to her prayer, you might say.

*(Paidir Ghobnait)**
A Dhia na Cruinne
Bí linn anseo.

Tabhair aire.
Bí a' faire
Anois 's go deo.
A Dhia, a bhronn orainn
Torthaí an tsaoil,
Bronn beannacht 's bua
Ar dheireadh mo scéal.

Next thing – though at first not much more
Than the hum of the chanter's drone –
The bees' humming swelled and swelled
To a mighty crescendo, full blown.

Those bees – may their honey be sweeter
Than syrup, or treacle or jam –
Spilled out of their hives, clouding the skies
With a magnificent, threatening swarm.

In a frenzy of buzzing and bizzing
Those bees – each carrying one sting –
Made a bee-line straight for the Creachaire's men
And hovered there – most menacing.

One little Bee – God bless it! –
Lit on the Creachaire's nose,
Looked straight in his eye as if to say
'Right! This is as far as yis goes!

These cattle belong to the people
Of Ballyvourney – they've little enough,
But we bees can give you "a little something" instead.'
Well! – that army just upped and ran off!

They took to their heels and ran for their life,
The Beachaire Rua had won,
And unless I'm very much mistaken
They're probably still on the run.

Ballyvourney is free now! Ballyvourney is free
From the terrible Creachaire Crua.
Ballyvourney is free, thanks 'bee' to God
And the prayer of the Beachaire Rua.

Listen, I know what you're thinking.
You don't believe me – *It's true!*
I saw it myself with my very own eyes.
It happened! It did! I'm telling you!

Footnotes

1   the people of Ballyvourney
2   cattle raider
3   red-haired bee-keeper
4   Gobnait, our friend

(Gobnait's Prayer)
Good God, Almighty,
Be with us this day.
Protect us and save us
From harm and dismay.
Dear God, our Creator,
From whom good things come,
May our story end happily
Before this day is done.

Chatting
Invite the children to chat to you about the story(ies).

Pupil Book
Invite the children to tell you about the pictures in the pupil book: *Alive-O* (Junior Infants/Primary One), pp. 22-23, 31; *Alive-O 3* (First Class/Primary Three), p. 7; *Alive-O 4* (Second Class/Primary Four), pp. 42-43.

Art
Invite the children to show you any artwork on the life of the saint that they may have completed. Chat to them about their work.

Video
Watch the piece of video relevant to St Brigid/Patrick: *Alive-O*, Saint Brigid, 'I Am Special'; *Alive-O 2*, Saint Patrick, 'New Life'. Chat to the children about what they see and hear.

Prayertime
Join with the children in a Prayertime in honour of the saint. A Prayertime on each saint is included below.

Alive-O (Junior Infants/Primary One)
Sign of the Cross

All
Saint Brigid of Ireland
Help us, we pray,
To be kind and loving
In our work and our play.

Leader
Brigid shows us how to share.

All
Blessed be Saint Brigid.

Leader
Brigid shows us how to love.

All
Blessed be Saint Brigid.

Leader
Brigid shows us how to be kind.

All
Blessed be Saint Brigid.

Saint Brigid of Ireland
Help us, we pray,
To be kind and loving
In our work and our play.

Sign of the Cross

Alive-O 2 (Senior Infants/Primary Two)
Sign of the Cross

Leader
Today we will thank God for sending Patrick to Ireland.

For Patrick's courage.

All
Thank you, God, for Patrick.

Leader
For Patrick's love of God.

All
Thank you, God, for Patrick.

Leader
For Patrick's care for others.

All
Thank you, God, for Patrick.

Leader
For all the work Patrick did to help others to know about God's love.

All
Thank you, God, for Patrick.

Sign of the Cross

Alive-O 3 (First Class/Primary Three)
Sign of the Cross

Leader *(as the candle is lit)*
We remember saints who shared the light of God's love in the world.
All over the world at this time of the year people remember saints who are special to them.
Many things and places are called after saints.
Our church is Saint _____. Our school is called after Saint _____.
Today, as we remember the saints, we ask them to pray for us.

All
Pray for us.

Leader
Saint Brigid.

All
Pray for us.

Leader
Saint Patrick.

All
Pray for us.

Leader
Saint Margaret.

All
Pray for us.

Add to the above list the names of any local saints that are known to the children. Some children in the class may also know the names of other saints.

Leader
Saint Columba (Colmcille).

All
Pray for us.

Leader
Glory be to the Father,
And to the Son,
And to the Holy Spirit.

All
As it was in the beginning,
Is now and ever shall be,
World without end. Amen.

Sign of the Cross

Alive-O 4 (Second Class/Primary Four)

Note: *For this Prayertime you will need a jar(s)/container(s) of honey. During the Prayertime the honey will be passed round for the children to taste. The candle you light for this Prayertime could be a beeswax candle.*

Sign of the Cross

Leader *(as the candle is lit)*
Spirit of Gobnait, guide me.
Courage of Gobnait, inspire me.
Peace of Gobnait, heal me.
Stillness of Gobnait, calm me.

We turn to Gobnait in prayer.
We ask her to pray for us.
We ask that our prayers to her may be as sweet as honey.

Pass the bowl(s)/container(s) of honey. Invite the children to dip in a finger and to 'taste' the honey. You might like to play the song 'Litany of the Saints' as this is happening.

Let us pray to St Gobnait.

All *(repeating after leader)*
Pray for us.

Leader
Saint Gobnait, keeper of bees.

All
Pray for us.

Leader
Saint Gobnait, woman of courage.

All
Pray for us.

Leader
Saint Gobnait, helper of the weak.

All
Pray for us.

Leader
Saint Gobnait, friend of the people.

All
Pray for us.

Leader
We ask Gobnait to help us to be quiet and still.

Close your eyes.
Feel the love of Gobnait surround you. *Pause*
Feel the love of Gobnait surround everyone in the class. *Pause*
Feel the love of Gobnait surround all those you love and care for. *Pause*

Let us pray together.

All
Glory be to the Father...

Sign of the Cross

Prayer forms an integral part of *Alive-O*. The children's faith in God is fostered through prayer and they can learn to express this faith in prayer. Children learn to pray by praying. For this reason the children are invited to pray with the teacher on a daily basis. The daily prayer usually focuses on the theme of the week's lesson. The children pray in many ways – by using the formal words of the Church, by singing, by hearing the Word of God in the Gospel, by praying in their own words. It is essential that young children develop from a very early age a sense that they can talk to God at any time and in any place and become secure in the knowledge that God is always listening and interested in what they have to say. Children learn by imitating the behaviour and action of significant adults around them. Likewise, with prayer, one of the best ways of teaching children to pray is to provide them with the opportunity to hear and to see adults pray. The daily Prayertimes provide the context for the class teacher to express her/his faith with the children.

As well as the daily Prayertimes, *Alive-O* provides three special Prayer Services each year where parents/guardians are invited to join in prayer with their children. These Prayer Services offer a context wherein children can listen to and witness their parents/guardians express their faith. As these Prayer Services are optional it is worth checking with the class teacher to see whether he/she would like to offer them to the parents/guardians. You might like to help plan and organise one of the services with the teacher and to encourage parents/guardians to attend. When handled creatively, the services can prove to be a wonderfully positive and prayerful experience for parents/ guardians, teachers and children alike. Participation in the services can help enhance relationships between children and their parents/guardians and between parish personnel and teachers. The Prayer Services usually happen on Day Five of the week, and just before the children are collected to go home. They are a culmination of the learning and reflection that the children have done during the week.

In order to help the reader gain an insight into the format of a Prayer Service, one Prayer Service for each of the four years is included here. The remaining Prayer Services may be found in the teacher's manuals.

Planning a Prayer Service
Some pointers that you might find helpful when planning a Prayer Service with the children:

* Read the Prayer Service as outlined in *Alive-O*. Being familiar with the context and the content will aid the flow of the service.

- Consult with the class teacher as to how the Prayer Service might be best organised and the most appropriate time to offer it.

- Check with the class teacher to see if any 'extra' items need to be brought in for the service.

- Encourage parents/guardians and other family members (e.g. grandparents) to attend if they are free. This could be announced during a Sunday liturgy or highlighted in the parish newsletter.

Junior Infants/Primary One: Term 1, Lesson 7 (*Alive-O*, p. 46)
Theme: Celebrating Change

This Prayer Service seeks to celebrate in ritual the child's leaving home, saying goodbye and starting school on the one hand and the parents'/ guardians' letting go, saying goodbye and waiting on the other. The Prayer Service is a way of marking the significance of the children's movement from home to school – their first step into the wider world.

Prayer Service
Teacher
Welcome, everyone, to this special little party. This party is about celebrating all the girls' and boys' having started school. We in school are very happy to have you with us and we hope that you will spend many happy days in our school. We also welcome you, parents/guardians, etc. The day a child starts school is a big day in the life of a parent/guardian as well as in the life of a child. It is a day when you feel a little bit sad and a little bit glad. Does this poem reflect your experience of that in any way?

Distribute copies of the poem 'Waiting' to the parents and guardians who are present. It is on p. 51 of Alive-O. *Then either read it, or have one of the parents/guardians read it, or play the tape.*

The children will now sing one of the songs they have learned about starting school. Feel free to play the tape in the background if you wish.

Child
This is a party. We have a big, big party-candle.

Teacher lights candle.

Leader
May this paschal candle light all our lives at home and in school and in church.

Child
In school there are many books. One special big book has our names in it.

Teacher calls the names.

As their names are called each child answers 'HERE I AM', or whatever has been decided during Lesson 2. Each child gets off his or her parent/guardian's lap or gently leaves their heart shape behind and joins a circle to wait until all the names have been called. When the last name has been called:

Child
At a party we sing songs. Let's all sing together. *(Children form a circle and sing* Monday Morning *or another song that they have learnt. Again feel free to play the tape in the background.)*

Leader
Let's watch a piece of video which tells the story of the weeks we have spent with the children since they started school. *(Play the first section of the video.)*

Parent or Teacher
We have another big book with lots of stories in it. Let's have a story. *(Parent reads the story* Miriam and Moses and Mum *as presented in the text. Children sit on the floor during the story.)*

Parent/Teacher – Introduction
This is a story about a baby called Moses who had to leave his mammy when he was a tiny baby. But he was okay because someone else arranged for him to be taken care of.

Miriam and Moses and Mum
Miriam was very happy and Miriam was very sad. She was happy because she had a new little baby brother. She was very sad because her mother said they would not be able to keep him. The king didn't allow Miriam's people to keep their baby boys. Miriam cried. Miriam's mammy cried and the baby cried too.

Then Miriam stopped crying. She got cross. 'We will just have to DO something,' she said to her mammy.

'You are right, Miriam,' her mammy replied.' We do not want our baby to go away from us. We must make a plan.' And that is what they did.

Miriam and her mammy made a special basket to keep the baby safe and warm. Then they wrapped him in a blanket and laid him in the basket because they could not keep him in their own house with them. They took the baby to the River Nile and they hid him in his basket among the tall rushes where no one would find him.

Then Miriam's mammy told her to hide nearby and keep watch over her little brother.

Now it was a very hot day and after a short time the king's daughter and her servants came to swim in the river. The princess spotted the basket in the rushes and sent one of her servants to see what was in it and to bring it to her.

Poor Miriam watched from her hiding-place. She didn't know what to do.

The princess looked into the basket and saw the baby. She knew he was one of the babies that her father, the king, did not allow. But the baby was crying and she felt sorry for him. 'I must find someone to look after him for me,' she said.

Just then Miriam jumped out of the bushes and ran to the princess, shouting, 'My mother is very good at minding babies, I could go and get her for you if you like.'

'Very well,' said the princess. 'But I must give him a name first. I will call him Moses because I pulled him out of the water.' Then the princess told Miriam's mammy to take the baby home and look after and feed him until he was a bit bigger. She gave her some money for minding him.

Miriam and her mammy were very happy. They had to let the baby go, but he had come back to them again. 'Phew! Thank God,' they said together.

Leader
Here we have some water. This water is blessed. I invite your parents/ guardians to take this water now and bless you, their child. *(Children return to their parents/guardians. The water is passed around. If some children are not accompanied by an adult, you could invite them to come forward so that you can bless them yourself.)*

Each parent/guardian blesses his or her child:
> In the name of the Father,
> And of the Son,
> And of the Holy Spirit,
> May God bless you
> and keep you safe
> in school and at home.

Child and Parent
Amen.

They give each other a hug.

Leader
The Lord be with you.

Participants
And also with you.

Leader
Deep peace of the running water to you.

Deep peace of the flowing air to you.
Deep peace of the quiet earth to you.
Deep peace of the shining stars to you.
Deep peace of the Son of peace to you.

Traditional Gaelic Rune

Participants
Amen.

The principal may like to thank participants.

You might like to have a small treat for each child as they leave for home.

Senior Infants/Primary Two: Term 2, Lesson 4 (*Alive-O 2*, p. 157)
Theme: Peace Within Me

This Prayer Service explores the notion of inner peace. It is through the children's capacity to create an inner space that they can be helped to become more deeply aware of God's presence in their lives. The Prayer Service reflects and celebrates this God-given peace through story/drama and song.

Prayer Service

Leader
In the name of the Father, and of the Son, and of the Holy Spirit. Amen. Peace be with you.

All
And also with you.

Leader
You are all very welcome to join us today as we pray for peace. First of all, we thank God for all the peace we have in our lives.

Child
For peaceful places.

All
Thank you, God, we pray.

Child
For people who help us to feel peaceful.

All
Thank you, God, we pray.

Child
For peaceful music.

All
Thank you, God, we pray.

Child
For peaceful colours.

All
Thank you, God, we pray.

Leader
We listen to a story about making peace.

Note: If the teacher has prepared a dramatisation of Jack and Jill *it could be included here. If not, you might like to read the story to the children and parents.*

Jack and Jill
Jack and Jill went up the hill
to fetch a pail of water.
Jack fell down and broke his crown
And Jill burst out with laughter.

And that is how the row between Jack and Jill began.

'Stop Jill,' cried Jack. 'Stop laughing at once.' But Jill could not stop laughing.

'It is not nice to laugh when someone has an accident,' he said, rubbing his sore head.

But Jill could not stop laughing.

'Very well then. Laugh if you want to,' said Jack, 'but you can fetch the pail of water yourself. I am not your friend anymore', and he picked himself up off the ground and marched off down the hill.

And so the row between Jack and Jill got worse.

'But Jack, you looked so funny,' Jill called after him. 'Don't be cross Jack. I couldn't help laughing.'

But Jack would not come back. So Jill picked up the bucket and filled it with water all by herself. The bucket was very heavy. It was difficult for Jill to carry it all by herself. As she was making her way down the hill, Jill slipped.

'Help!' she shouted, as she tumbled all the way down the hill. By the time she reached the bottom, her clothes were all wet and covered in mud.

Now it was Jack's turn to laugh.

'Stop Jack,' cried Jill. 'Stop laughing at once.'

'It is not nice to laugh when someone has an accident,' she said.

But Jack could not stop laughing.

'Very well then, Jack,' said Jill, 'laugh if you want to, but you can just go **back** up the hill and fetch **another** pail of water all by yourself. I am not your friend anymore.' She sat down at the bottom of the hill to wait for the sun to dry her clothes.

And so the row between Jack and Jill continued.

'But Jill, you looked so funny,' laughed Jack. 'Don't be cross Jill, I couldn't help laughing.'

Now Jack picked up the empty bucket and set off, up the hill to fetch the water. Jack was doing very well. He would have reached the top of the hill in no time at all, except that the spilt water had made the ground slippery. Just when he had reached the top of the hill, Jack fell down AGAIN! Oh dear. And what do you think Jill did? You are right. Jill laughed and laughed and laughed.

Now this row between Jack and Jill looked as though it might go on for ever and ever. Oh dear. What could these two do to make peace between them? *(The teacher/priest might pause here to allow the children to make some suggestions as to how Jack and Jill could make peace with each other.)*

Jack and Jill's father was getting worried about the two children. 'They should be back by now,' he thought to himself. 'I had better go out and see what has happened to them.' When he reached the hill he saw Jack and Jill, sitting at the bottom with their backs to each other. They would not look at each other, or talk to each other, or help each other, or be friends with each other.

'Jack laughed at me,' said Jill crossly.

'She laughed at me first,' said Jack.

'Stop, stop, stop,' their father called. 'This fighting will get us nowhere. We need to make peace instead of fighting.'

'But we don't know how to make peace,' said Jack and Jill.

'It is easy,' said their father. 'First you must tell each other that you are sorry. You must say that you won't do this again and then you can shake hands. That is a sign that you are friends and that you will end your fighting.' And that is how the row between Jack and Jill was ended.

So now
When Jack and Jill go up the hill
To fetch a pail of water,
They help each other all the way,
They're best friends ever after.

Leader
We pray that we will always be able to be at peace with those around us.

Child
With those at home.

All
God, give us peace.

Child
With those at school.

All
God, give us peace.

Child
With those in our neighbourhood.

All
God, give us peace.

Leader
Close your eyes...
Settle yourself comfortably in your seat...
Place your feet on the floor...
And your hands comfortably in your lap...

Think of a place where you usually feel peaceful. Somewhere in your home or in the outside world. Imagine the place in your mind.

Imagine that you are there now. Feel the peace that you usually feel in that place. Peace all over your body... in your feet... your legs... your tummy... your chest... your hands... your arms... your head. Enjoy the feeling. Finally, feel that peace inside in your inside world.

Give thanks to God for peace.
If you can't feel that peace right now that's OK. God is still with you. God is always with you. Talk to God about how you feel right now. Ask God to bless you with peace soon.

As you open your eyes prepare to offer a sign of peace to the other people gathered here.

(Encourage people to move freely around the room offering each other a sign of peace.)

Note: *If the children have made a peace card, proceed as stated below. Alternatively, move from the Sign of Peace to the final song.*

Leader
We now invite the children to come forward and take the peace card they have made and give it to someone to take away.

Let this card remind us to make peace.

All *(sing)*
Song of Peace

You might like to invite a parent/guardian to read the reflection entitled 'Peace', which is on p. 166 of Alive-O 2.

Leader
As we come to the end
of our prayer service
we ask God to bless us with peace.

The Lord bless you and keep you.

The Lord make his face shine upon you and be gracious to you.
The Lord lift up his countenance upon you and give you his peace.

All
Amen.

First Class/Primary Three: Term 2, Lesson 3 (*Alive-O 3*, p. 182)
Theme: We Are The Greatest

This Prayer Service seeks to celebrate the particular perspective on childhood that was given by Jesus. During the week the children have learnt to acknowledge, to express and to celebrate the goodness of childhood and to find joy in it. The Prayer Service honours the goodness that Jesus saw in all people and especially in children.

Prayer Service
Sign of the Cross

All *(sing)*
We are the Greatest

Leader
When Jesus was asked who was the greatest he pointed to a child. Today we celebrate the greatness of children.

Each child has a baptismal candle. (You might like to use a simple night-light type candle if the baptismal candle is not available.)

The children come forward carrying their unlit candles, and the leader lights them from the main candle.

Child *(with help from the leader if necessary, while placing the candle around the main candle)*
I am a child.
Jesus said that children are the greatest in God's kingdom.

Leader (Reading)
We are the Greatest
Today is Market Day. The children love Market Day. They go to the town square. All the grown-ups are there. There are men selling cheeses. There are women buying cloth. There are bakers selling bread. There are people buying spices and fruit. There are cows mooing and donkeys braying and goats baaing. The Market Place is busy. The Market Place is noisy. The Market Place is a busy place for the adults. It is a place of fun for the children. They love to run about and enjoy being with their friends. They play hide-and-seek among the adults.

Today a man comes to the Market Place. At first no one notices the man. He sits in the middle of the square where everyone will be able to see him. He speaks in a loud voice so that everyone will be able to hear him. He tells those who stop and listen about a kingdom. He calls it the Kingdom of God. He says that in God's kingdom everyone is happy. In God's kingdom everyone loves their friends as well as those who are not their friends.

171

'What kind of place is this kingdom,' say some of the grown-ups, 'where people love those who are not their friends?'

'How can we get to live in such a place?' say some others.

'God's kingdom is not any particular place,' says the man. 'God's kingdom can be anywhere. Wherever people love one another, wherever people are kind and gentle, wherever people share with one another, that is where God's kingdom is. God's kingdom can be right here, right now.'

'I have a question for you,' says one man. 'In our community I am an important person. I would like to know who is the most important person in this Kingdom of God that you talk about.'

Now the Market Place grows quiet. The noise stops. The buying and selling stops. The children notice that everything has gone quiet too. The children go on playing. From where they are they can see the crowd of people gathered around the man.

'What's happening?' some of the children ask each other.

Just then the man comes over to the children. He says, 'Who will help me? I need one of you to help me teach the grown-ups something very important.'

'Me, me, me!' say the children. The man smiles. He takes the smallest child by the hand. He takes the child into the middle of the crowd. He wants everyone to notice the child.

'You ask me who is the most important person in God's kingdom,' says the man to the crowd. 'I will tell you now,' he says. 'Do you see this little child? I tell you, the child is the greatest in God's kingdom.'

A murmur of shock and surprise runs through the crowd of grown-ups. They can hardly believe their eyes. They can hardly believe their ears. The child! The child is the greatest in God's kingdom! They have never heard the like of this before!

When the man is finished the child runs back to the other children.

'What did the man want?'; 'What did the man say?'; 'What did the man teach the people?' they ask the child.

'He taught them that children are the greatest,' the child answers. The children clap and cheer.

'Who is this man?' the children ask.

'His name is Jesus,' the child answers.

'Hurrah for Jesus!' the children shout. 'Hurrah, hurrah, hurrah!'

All *(sing)*
We are the Greatest

Leader
We will now listen to the reflection.

You might like to invite a parent/guardian to read the reflection entitled 'Why is it, Lord' which is on p. 194 of Alive-O 3.

Leader
We now invite each child to go to her or his parent/guardian (or whoever is accompanying the child) to hear why they are the greatest. Parents, you can whisper in your child's ear so no one else can hear. Then, bless your child, making the Sign of the Cross. Those whose parents/guardians are unable to be here today can come to the teacher who will tell them why they are the greatest and bless them with holy water.

The children then go to the appropriate adult, who, having whispered in their ear why they are the greatest, makes the Sign of the Cross on their forehead with holy water.

Invite the children to put on their 'We are the Greatest!' badges.

Applause

Leader
We pray together.

All
Glory be to the Father...

Leader
As we go away from here we ask God to bless us and keep us safe.

All
May the Lord bless us and keep us.
May he let his face shine upon us and be gracious to us.
May he look upon us with kindness and give us his peace.
Amen.

Sign of the Cross

Second Class/Primary Four: Term 3, Lesson 11 (*Alive-O 4*, p. 421)
Theme: Time to Go – Alive-O!

This Prayer Service celebrates the completion of the school year in story, song and praise of God.

Prayer Service
Sign of the Cross

All *(sing)*
Alive-O

Leader
You are all very welcome here today as we celebrate the end of our year together. It is a special day, because it is our last day in this class. We have been together all year long. Maybe we are excited to know that the summer holidays are here. Maybe we feel sad because some of us will be saying goodbye to each other for a while. But it is a good day because we have a lot to be thankful for.

Let us light our candle.

Let us close our eyes and in the silence of our hearts give thanks for the year that has passed. We will pray the words: 'Praise to you, Lord Jesus Christ'.

Close your eyes.
Still your body.
Feel your breath as it flows in and out of your body.
Feel your breath as it enters your nostrils. *(Pause)*

Feel your breath as it travels all the way to your lungs, bringing life to every part of your body. *(Pause)*
Feel your breath as it leaves your body, as it gently flows out of your nostrils. *(Pause)*

Listen to your breath for a little while as it gets slower and slower.
Today we will pray the words to Jesus: 'Praise to you, Lord Jesus Christ'.
As you breathe in pray with your inside voice that no one else can hear: 'Praise to you'.
As you breathe out pray: 'Lord Jesus Christ'.
Pray the words gently to yourself every time you breathe in and out. Don't be in a hurry.
God is with you as you pray the words. *(Pause)*

When you feel that everyone is ready:
Gently open your eyes.
Let us ask God's blessing on us all as we pray:

All

God be with us on our way.

Leader

We ask God to bless us and to keep us safe during the summer holidays.

All

God be with us on our way.

Leader

As we say goodbye to this classroom.

All

God be with us on our way.

Leader

As we say goodbye to each other.

All

God be with us on our way.

Leader

As we begin our summer holidays.

All

God be with us on our way.

Leader

We have had a good year together.
Let us thank God now for all that we have learned.

For songs to sing. Let us sing a favourite song now.

All

Song of children's choice

Thank you, God, for songs to sing.

Leader

For stories/poems to tell. Let us tell a story/poem now.

All

Story/poem of children's choice

Thank you, God, for stories/poems to tell.

Leader

For games to play. Let us play a game now.

All

Game of children's choice

Thank you, God, for games to play.

Leader
For mimes and plays to act out. Let us act out a mime or a favourite part of a play.

All
Mime/part of play of children's choice

Thank you, God, for the fun of acting.

Leader
Thank you, God, for everything that we learned this year.
Thank you for the gift of each other.
May God bless us and keep us safe.

All
Amen.

Leader
May God bless our families and friends.

Invite the children to turn to their parents/guardians beside them and wish them God's blessing by saying 'May God bless you always'.

All
Amen.

Invite a parent/guardian to read the reflection 'A Parent's Blessing' which is on p. 429 of Alive-O 4.

Leader
May God bless each and every one as we make the Sign of the Cross.

All
In the name of the Father,
And of the Son,
And of the Holy Spirit.
Amen.

All *(sing)*
Alive-O

Sign of the Cross

Section Five: Sacramental Catechesis

Children are introduced to and prepared for the reception of some sacraments in our primary schools. Teachers work creatively and diligently with the children and watch them grow in understanding and knowledge of the importance of sacraments as they move through the primary school. Sacramental preparation, however, is best seen in the context of the entire year, which seeks to lay the foundation to an understanding of sacramental sign, symbol and ritual. *Alive-O 3* and *Alive-O 4* invite the children in a particular way to participate in a series of lessons that specifically prepare them for their first reception of the sacraments of Eucharist and Reconciliation. The children are also introduced to an understanding of the sacrament of Baptism. You might like to give support to the teacher in her/his exploration of the sacraments with the children. A visit to the classroom and chatting with the children about a particular sacrament is one way in which this support can be offered. To facilitate such a visit a brief outline of the approach adopted for each sacrament is given below. Suggestions for interaction with the children will then be made. For greater detail please refer to the relevant teacher's manual.

Sacrament of Baptism

The Holy Spirit is the Spirit of God, the third person of the Blessed Trinity. Each year *Alive-O* seeks to heighten the children's awareness of the presence of God's Spirit moving at the heart of all life. They are helped to reflect on how the Spirit of God is active in the world of nature and can be seen in the changing seasons and in the beauty of the world. They see how the same Spirit is active in the life of Jesus, in his efforts to make God present and active in the world.

In *Alive-O 3* (Term 3, Lesson 6: 'Holy Spirit Help Us') the children are introduced to the story of Pentecost. Jesus promised his followers that the Holy Spirit would help them to remember all that he had taught them and would help them to live as he had asked them to. The Holy Spirit came to the apostles at Pentecost. The Holy Spirit comes to us in Baptism. The children reflect on the qualities of the Holy Spirit: love, joy, peace, patience, kindness, goodness, truthfulness, gentleness, trustfulness and self-control.

The following year, *Alive-O 4* (Term 3, Lesson 9: 'The Spirit of God in Us') continues to help the children come to an understanding of the sacrament of Baptism. The specific baptismal symbols are explored – water, oil, light and white shawl. The children are also introduced to the Rite of Baptism.

If you choose to visit the class during this period (sometime after Easter), you might like to focus on some of the following:

Song
Ask the children to sing one of the songs that they are learning. Alternatively, you could sing a song for them. *Come Holy Spirit* (*Alive-O 3*, p. 327 and *Alive-O 4*, p. 405); *Song of Baptism* (*Alive-O 4*, p. 406). The songs are available in the teacher's manual and on CD/tape. Chat to the children about the words of the song.

Story
Read or invite the children to tell the story of Pentecost (*Alive-O 3*, p. 322; *Alive-O 4*, p. 404).

Chatting
Chatting about the stories: Can you remember a time when you missed someone who had gone away? Why did you miss them? What kind of things did you miss? Jesus' friends missed him. What special things about their friend do you think they missed most? How do you think the Holy Spirit helped Jesus' friends? How can the Holy Spirit help you? Have you ever been to a Baptism? Tell us about it.

Pupil Book
Chat to the children about the pictures and text on page 44 of *Alive-O 3* and page 41 of *Alive-O 4*.

Video
Alive-O 4 has a section on a baptismal ceremony. You might like to watch it with the children and chat to them about what they see and hear.

Sacrament of Reconciliation

Alive-O seeks to put the children in touch with their own individual goodness and with the collective goodness that is at the heart of human nature. The Christian tradition has always balanced 'love of oneself' with the active 'love of one's neighbour'. Built into Jesus' command to 'love your neighbour as yourself' is an intrinsic respect for one's own uniqueness, one's own being. Yet love for oneself cannot be separated from our love and compassion for one another and for God. Made in the image and likeness of God we reflect something of the goodness of God. Jesus is the one who above all embodied the full potential of that human goodness and who revealed what the goodness of God is like. Time and again this was reflected in Jesus' ability to connect with the very heart of those whom he met, in his unique way of being with others, in his attitude to the poor, in the stories he told and in the love he had for God. It is in this context that *Alive-O* situates the sacrament of Reconciliation.

In preparing the children for the sacrament the teacher helps them to begin the process of reconciliation whereby they:

(i)   come to recognise their essential goodness and rejoice in it;
(ii) appreciate their interrelatedness with others;
(iii) become aware of and acknowledge their own failures and sinfulness;
(iv) say sorry for the times when their behaviour has caused pain or hurt and has weakened the connection between themselves and others and between themselves and God.

In this way the children become aware of the steps necessary for reconciliation to take place. This process of reconciliation is set in the context of the secure knowledge of the never-ending love of God for each one of them, in spite of failure on their part. This process begins in *Alive-O 3* and is continued in *Alive-O 4*.

Specific preparation for the sacrament of Reconciliation usually occurs over a series of lessons in Term Two – after Christmas and before Easter. If you choose to visit First and Second Class (Primary Three and Primary Four) during this period you might like to tap into some of the following:

Song
Ask the children to sing one of the following songs. Alternatively, you might like to sing a song for/with them. The songs are available in the teacher's manuals and on CD/tape.

Alive-O 3	*Alive-O 4*
Beings, p. 180	*Being Connected,* p. 198
We Thank You, God, We Do, p. 181	*Sanctus,* p. 213
We are the Greatest, p. 192	*The Lost Sheep,* p. 234
The Lost Sheep, p. 214	*My Shepherd is the Lord,* p. 236
I'm Sorry, p. 226	*The Way to Be,* p. 248
I'm Sorry, God, p. 237	*I'm Sorry, God,* p. 263
The King of Love, p. 251	*I'm Sorry,* p. 282

Story
Invite the children to tell one of the following stories. The story the children may tell will vary according to the time of year you visit the class. The stories are available in the teacher's manuals.

Alive-O 3	*Alive-O 4*
We Are the Greatest, pp. 185/240	*Jairus' Rejoices,* p. 212
The Good Shepherd, pp. 208/242/282	*Sheep and Shepherd Celebrate,* p. 232

Chatting
Chat to the children about the story.

Pupil Book

Chat to the children about the pictures and text on some of the following pages: 25, 26, 28, 30, 31, 32 of *Alive-O 3* (First Class/Primary Three) and 24, 25, 27, 28, 29 of *Alive-O 4* (Second Class/Primary Four).

Video

Watch the video pieces 'We are the Greatest' and 'The Lost Sheep' with First Class/Primary Three *(Alive-O 3)* and the sections on the dramatisation of the story *Jairus Rejoices* and *The Good Shepherd* with Second Class/Primary Four *(Alive-O 4)*.

The Rite for Reconciliation (Rite 1 and Rite 2) is included in the teacher's manual *Alive-O 3* (pp. 244-351) and *Alive-O 4* (pp. 268-276). *Alive-O 4* also includes a section called 'Getting Ready for the celebration of First Penance' (pp. 439-443). These guidelines, while primarily directed to the class teacher, may prove helpful when planning and discussing the celebration with the class and their teacher.

Sacrament of the Eucharist

Throughout each year *Alive-O* endeavours to explore with the children the values and attitudes that are central to an understanding of and a meaningful participation in Eucharistic celebration, i.e.

- An ability to work with symbol and to take part in ritual;
- A sense of being-with-others;
- A sense of coming together with others;
- Listening to the Word of God;
- A sense of gratitude and thanksgiving;
- A sense of the meaning of celebration;
- An ability to reflect on the life, death and resurrection of Jesus Christ;
- A capacity to forgive and be forgiven;
- A sense of God's presence in sign and sacrament.

Catechesis on the Eucharist is integrated into the entire year. However, there are specific lessons in *Alive-O 3* and *Alive-O 4* that prepare the children for their first reception of Holy Communion by exploring the following fundamental aspects of the Mass:

- The Christian community gathers together;
- Listening to the Word of God; sharing story;
- Remembering Jesus' love for us; sharing memories;
- Giving thanks;
- Celebrating the forgiveness of God our Father;
- Sharing the Bread of life; sharing food/meals;
- Going in peace to be like Jesus; sharing life.

Specific preparation for the sacrament of the Eucharist usually takes place over a series of lessons in Term Three, though some teachers may begin the preparation before Easter. If you choose to visit First or Second Class (Primary Three or Primary Four) during this period you might like to tap into the following:

Songs
Ask the children to sing one of the following songs. Alternatively, you might like to sing a song for/with them. The songs are available in the teacher's manuals and on CD/tape.

Alive-0 3	*Alive-O 4*
Once Upon a Time, pp. 99/284	*Happy in the Presence*, p. 325
Happy in the Presence of the Lord, p. 285	*This is the Day*, p. 327
Eat This Bread, p. 298	*Listen*, p. 339
Céad Míle Fáilte Romhat, p. 297	*Love!*, p. 350
I Remember, p. 309	*We Come to You, Lord Jesus*, p. 360
Do this in Memory of Jesus, p. 318	*Blessed Be God*, p. 362
	Céad Míle Fáilte Romhat, p. 382
	Eat this Bread, p. 383
	I am the Bread, p. 384
	Do this in Memory, p. 393
	Go Now in Peace, p. 395

Stories
Invite the children to tell one of the following stories. The story the children will tell will vary according to the time of year you visit the classroom. The stories are available in the teacher's manuals.

Alive-0 3	*Alive-O 4*
The Market Place, p. 277	*The Passover*, p. 323
The Parable of the Sower, p. 93/281	*The Crucifixion*, pp. 292/348
The Good Shepherd, p. 208/242/282	*The Ten Lepers*, p. 359
The Last Supper, p. 254/293	*Father Forgive Them*, p. 371
A Special Meal, p. 305	*The Last Supper*, p. 285/381
Jesus Visits Three Special Friends, p. 312	

Chatting
Chat to the children about the story.

Pupil Book
Chat to the children about the pictures and text on pages 39, 40, 41, 42, 43 of *Alive-O 3* (First Class/Primary Three) and pages 34, 35, 36, 37, 38, 39, 40 of *Alive-O 4* (Second Class/Primary Four).

Video

Watch the video piece 'Mass' with First Class/Primary Three *(Alive-O 3)* or 'Visit to the Church' with Second Class/Primary Four *(Alive-O 4)*. Chat to the children about what they see and hear.

The preparation of the children for First Communion is an exciting and challenging task. It is the combined responsibility of the home, school and parish. To help maximise the participation and involvement of the relevant parties in all aspects of the children's preparations for First Communion *Alive-O 4* offers 'Getting Ready for the First Communion Celebration' guidelines *(Alive-O 4,* p. 444-448). These guidelines consist of a series of pointers or suggestions that school and parish personnel may find useful when planning this event.

Alive-O 4 also includes an example of a First Communion celebration (pp. 449-462). This outline is not offered in any prescriptive way and can be adapted and changed according to the needs and preferences of each parish or school. The preparation and planning of this event provide an excellent opportunity for parish, home and school to work in partnership towards providing a positive and spiritual experience of both Church and sacrament for young children.

Section Six: Liturgical Links

Religious education is most effective when school, home and parish work side by side. Often, however, the home and the parish feel isolated from what is happening in the school. Likewise, the school often feels that the task of educating the children in the Christian faith is left entirely to its teachers. Aware of the need to connect the parish and home with the events of the school, *Alive-O* developed *At Home with Alive-O* and *Alive-O Liturgical Links*. Both these 'packs' contain sheets that can be photocopied and used in either the home or the parish. *At Home with Alive-O* is directed to the home and aims to give parents/guardians an insight into what their children are learning in school and to provide them with some resource materials so that they can continue at home what the teacher has begun in school. *Alive-O Liturgical Links* on the other hand is directed at the parish. Initiated in *Alive-O 3* and continued in *Alive-O 4*, these sheets are intended to provide priests and parish personnel with materials from *Alive-O* that may be used in the Sunday liturgy or in the parish newsletter. All the above material is available in the *Alive-O* kit's Resource Pack.

Taking the themes that have already been selected for inclusion in this compilation, some suggestions are being offered below by way of helping to connect the school and parish. However, every parish is different and the suggestions indicated are merely pointers to what may be possible at parish level. For more detailed suggestions, see the Resource Pack in *Alive-O 3* and *Alive-O 4*.

September

The children begin a new school year. Some children return to school after the long summer holidays. Some children on the other hand begin school for the first time. To mark the beginning of the new school year for the children and for the parish you might like to:

- welcome the children back to school on the first Sunday of the month and give a blessing for the new year;
- have your parish newsletter make reference to the children beginning school for the first time;
- ask the choir to learn one of the songs that the children learn at the beginning of the year. The song could be from *Alive-O, Alive-O 2, Alive-O 3* or *Alive-O 4;*
- have an Enrolment Ceremony for the children who will be celebrating their First Penance and First Communion later in the year;
- invite the community to pray for the children as they prepare for the reception of the sacraments.

November

During the month of November the children reflect on the Feast of All Saints and All Souls. In the parish you might like to:

- make reference to what the children are doing in school in the Sunday liturgy;
- display some of the artwork that the children have completed during this month;
- ask the community to pray for the dead during the coming weeks;
- plan a parish visit to the local graveyard. Invite the parishioners to lay a wreath and to say a prayer around their family grave(s);
- ask the choir to learn the song *Remember*.

Advent

In school the children hear the Advent stories: The Annunciation and The Visitation. In the parish you might like to:

- remind the community on the First Sunday of Advent that the school children are beginning their preparations for the celebration of the birth of Jesus;
- display an Advent wreath;
- use some of the Advent prayers that the children are learning during the Advent season;
- ask the choir to learn some of the Advent songs that the children are learning at school.

Christmas

In school the children hear the Christmas story: The birth of Jesus. In the parish you might like to:

- refer to this in the Sunday liturgy;
- ask the children to present the dramatisation of the Christmas story for the Christmas Eve/Day liturgy;
- ask the choir to learn some of the Christmas songs that the children are learning;
- invite some classes to display their Christmas artwork in the church.

Lent

In school First and Second Class (Primary Three and Primary Four) begin their preparations for the season of Lent. In the parish you might like to:

- make reference to this in the Sunday liturgy;
- ask the choir to learn some of the Lenten songs that the children are learning;

- create a Lenten 'wilderness' in the church in line with the *Alive-O 3* 'Little Wilderness';
- ask the community to pray for the children who are getting ready for First Penance;
- display the names of the children who will be making their First Penance in the church or in the parish newsletter.

Easter

In school the children hear the Easter stories. In the parish you might like to:

- invite the children to participate in the Stations of the Cross on Good Friday;
- display some of the children's drawings of some of the Stations of the Cross;
- ask the choir to learn some of the songs that the children are learning for this season;
- create an Easter display. Ask some classes to help in the creation of this;
- invite some children to act out the Resurrection story on Easter Sunday morning or at the Vigil Mass;
- alert the community to the forthcoming celebration of some children's First Communion;
- ask the community to remember the children in their prayers as they get ready for the great event;
- display the names of the children who will be receiving their First Communion in the church or in the parish newsletter.

Mary

In school the children make a May altar and remember the significant moments in the life of Mary. In the parish you might like to:

- decorate or invite the class to decorate an altar to Mary in the church;
- ask the choir to learn some of the songs that the children are learning to celebrate Mary as the mother of God's Son;
- display some of the children's Mary cards in the church;
- invite the congregation to say the *Hail Mary*. Ask some children to pray the *Hail Mary* using the actions.

Liturgical Year and Sunday Readings

Each year the children hear a number of biblical readings. Some of these readings are heard during the Sunday liturgies. The following grid outlines the link between the stories that the children hear in school and the Sunday readings. In some instances the children will have heard the entire Gospel story. In other instances they may have heard only part of the reading. When planning the Sunday liturgy or, indeed, a children's liturgy, it might be useful to make note of the readings with which the children are familiar. It is important to note that the children hear adapted and abridged versions of the biblical readings in *Alive-O* and *Alive-O 2*. However, *Alive-O 3* and *Alive-O 4*, while continuing to offer simplified versions of the stories to the children, also offer the children the opportunity to hear the readings direct from the Bible.

	Cycle A	Cycle B	Cycle C
4th Sunday of Advent		Luke 1: 26-38 *Alive-O 3* *Alive-O 4*	Luke 1: 39-45 *Alive-O 2* *Alive-O 3* *Alive-O 4*
Christmas			
Midnight Mass	Luke 2:1-14 *Alive-O 4*	Luke 2:1-14 *Alive-O 4*	Luke 2:1-14 *Alive-O 4*
Dawn Mass	Luke 2:15-20 *Alive-O* *Alive-O 2* *Alive-O 3* *Alive-O 4*	Luke 2:15-20 *Alive-O* *Alive-O 2* *Alive-O 3* *Alive-O 4*	Luke 2:15-20 *Alive-O* *Alive-O 2* *Alive-O 3* *Alive-O 4*
Holy Family	————	Luke 2:22-40 *Alive-O* *Alive-O 3*	Luke 2:41-52 *Alive-O 3*
Mary, Mother of God (1 Jan)	Luke 2:16-21 *Alive-O* *Alive-O 2* *Alive-O 3* *Alive-O 4*	Luke 2:16-21 *Alive-O* *Alive-O 2* *Alive-O 3* *Alive-O 4*	Luke 2:16-21 *Alive-O* *Alive-O 2* *Alive-O 3* *Alive-O 4*
Epiphany (6 Jan)	Matthew 2:1-12 *Alive-O 4*	Matthew 2:1-12 *Alive-O 4*	Matthew 2:1-12 *Alive-O 4*
5th Sunday in in Ordinary Time	————	Mark 1:29-39 *Alive-O 4*	————
3rd Sunday of Lent	John 4:5-42 *Alive-O 3*	————	————

	Cycle A	Cycle B	Cycle C
Passion Sunday	Matthew 26:14-27:66	_____	Luke 22:14-23:56
	Alive-O 3		*Alive-O 3*
	Alive-O 4		*Alive-O 4*
Easter Vigil	Matthew 28:1-10	Mark 16:1-8	Luke 24:1-12
	Alive-O	*Alive-O*	*Alive-O*
	Alive-O 2	*Alive-O 2*	*Alive-O 2*
	Alive-O 3	*Alive-O 3*	*Alive-O 3*
3rd Sunday of Easter	_____	_____	John 21:1-19
			Alive-O 4
Pentecost Sunday	Acts 2:1-11	Acts 2:1-11	Acts 2:1-11
	Alive-O 3	*Alive-O 3*	*Alive-O 3*
	Alive-O 4	*Alive-O 4*	*Alive-O 4*
Corpus Christi	_____	Mark 14:12-16; 22-26	Luke 9:11-17
		Alive-O 3	*Alive-O 3*
		Alive-O 4	*Alive-O 4*
Sacred Heart	_____	_____	Luke 15:3-7
			Alive-O 3
			Alive-O 4
11th Sunday in Ordinary Time	_____	Mark 4:26-34	_____
		Alive-O 3	
13th Sunday in Ordinary Time	_____	Mark 5:21-43	_____
		Alive-O 4	
15th Sunday in Ordinary Time	Matthew 13:1-23	_____	_____
	Alive-O 3		
16th Sunday in Ordinary Time	_____	Luke 10:38-42	_____
		Alive-O 3	
17th Sunday in Ordinary Time	_____	John 6:1-15	Luke 11:1-13
		Alive-O 3	*Alive-O 3*
		Alive-O 4	
18th Sunday in Ordinary Time	Matthew 14:13-21	_____	_____
	Alive-O 3		
	Alive-O 4		

	Cycle A	Cycle B	Cycle C
24th Sunday in Ordinary Time	_____	_____	Luke 15:1-32 *Alive-O 3* *Alive-O 4*
25th Sunday in Ordinary Time	_____	Mark 9:30-37 *Alive-O 3*	_____
28th Sunday in Ordinary Time	_____	_____	Luke 17:11-19 *Alive-O 4*
Christ the King	_____	John 18:33-37 *Alive-O 4*	Luke 23:35-43 *Alive-O 4*

Formal Prayers

The children learn the following formal prayers of the Christian community.

	Junior Infants/Primary One	Senior Infants/Primary Two	First Class/Primary Three	Second Class/Primary Four
Sign of the Cross	Yes	Yes	Yes	Yes
Our Father		Yes	Yes	Yes
Hail Mary		Yes	Yes	Yes
Glory be to the Father	Yes	Yes	Yes	Yes
Morning Prayer	Yes	Yes	Yes	Yes
Night Prayer	Yes	Yes	Yes	Yes
Prayer to Jesus			Yes	Yes
Prayer to the Trinity			Yes	Yes
Prayers to the Holy Spirit			Yes	Yes
Prayer to Mary			Yes	Yes
Journey Prayer			Yes	Yes
Grace before Meals	Yes	Yes	Yes	Yes
Grace after Meals	Yes	Yes	Yes	Yes
Act of Sorrow			Yes	Yes
Prayer for Forgiveness			Yes	Yes
Prayer after Forgiveness			Yes	Yes
Mass Responses			Yes	Yes
Confiteor			Yes	Yes
Prayer before Communion			Yes	Yes
Prayer after Communion			Yes	Yes

Scripture Stories

The following grid outlines the biblical stories that the children, through *Alive-O,* come to love and tell.

	Junior Infants/Primary One	Senior Infants/Primary Two	First Class/Primary Three	Second Class/Primary Four
Birth of Moses Ex 2:1-10	Yes			
Exodus Story: The Passover Ex 15:22-25	Yes		Yes	Yes
Call of David I Sam 16:19-22	Yes			
The Anointing of David 2 Sam 5:1-3				Yes
The Annunciation Lk 1:26-38			Yes	Yes
The Visitation Lk 1:39-56		Yes	Yes	Yes
The Birth of Jesus Lk 2:1-20; Mt 2:1-12	Yes	Yes	Yes	Yes
The Presentation in the Temple Lk 2:25-37, 36-38	Yes		Yes	Yes
Finding of Jesus in the Temple Lk 2:41-50			Yes	Yes
Calling of the Apostles Mt 4:18-22; Mk 1:16-20; Lk 5:1-11				Yes
Story of Mary, Martha and Lazarus Lk 10:38-41			Yes	Yes

	Junior Infants/Primary One	Senior Infants/Primary Two	First Class/Primary Three	Second Class/Primary Four
Jesus and the Desert Lk 4:1; Mk 1:12				Yes
Jesus Teaches How to Pray Lk 11:1-4			Yes	
Who is the Greatest: Jesus and the Children Lk 9:46-48			Yes	Yes
Jesus and the Woman at the Well Jn 4:7-14			Yes	
Healing of Peter's Mother-in-law Mk 1:29-39; Lk 4:38-39			Yes	
Jairus' Daughter Mk 5:21-24, 35-43			Yes	Yes
Ten Lepers Lk 17:11-19				Yes
The Loaves and Fish Lk 9:10-16; Jn 6:10-15			Yes	Yes
Parable of the Lost Sheep/Good Shepherd Lk 15:3-7			Yes	Yes
Parable of the Yeast Mk 13:4-9			Yes	
Parable of the Lost Coin Lk 15:8-9			Yes	
Parable of the Sower Mk 4:1-9; Mt 13:4-10			Yes	
The Last Supper Mk 14:22-26; Lk 22:19-20			Yes	Yes

	Junior Infants/Primary One	Senior Infants/Primary Two	First Class/Primary Three	Second Class/Primary Four
The Passion and Death of Jesus Lk 23			Yes	Yes
Women at the Tomb Lk 24:1-12; Mk 16:1-8	Yes	Yes	Yes	
Risen Jesus at Lake Tiberius Jn 21:1-19				Yes
The Pentecost Story Acts 2:1-11			Yes	Yes